Ford and **McRae**

Other books by this author include:

FORMULA ONE UNCOVERED
The other side of the track

MICHAEL SCHUMACHER
Formula for success

Ford and McRae

Focus on the World Rally Championship

by **Derick Allsop** Foreword by Colin McRae

First published in November 1999

Photography by McKlein, Les Kolczak and LAT Photographic, courtesy Ford.

British Library Cataloguing in Publication Data:
A catalogue record for this book is available from the British Library

ISBN 1 85960 656 3

Library of Congress catalog card no. 99-75337

Haynes North America, Inc.
861 Lawrence Drive, Newbury Park,
California 91320, USA

Haynes Publishing, Sparkford, Nr Yeovil, Somerset, BA22 7JJ.
Tel: 01963 440635 Fax: 01963 440001
Int. tel: +44 1963 440635 Fax: +44 1963 440001
E-mail: sales@haynes-manuals.co.uk
Web site: www.haynes.co.uk

Designed & typeset by G&M, Raunds, Northamptonshire, England
Printed and bound by Imprimerie Pollina s.a., Luçon, France n° 78440

Contents

Acknowledgements

Rallying is a team effort and so is this book. It could not have been produced without the assistance and forbearance of everyone involved with the Ford Martini operation: Martin Whitaker and his colleagues at Ford, Malcolm Wilson, Guenther Steiner, the engineers, mechanics, caterers and staff at M-Sport. My thanks to all of them. I am especially grateful for the co-operation of Colin McRae and the other drivers and co-drivers – Nicky Grist, Thomas Rådström, Simon Jean-Joseph, Petter Solberg, Fred Gallagher and Phil Mills. I wish also to thank Gavin Green of Ford, Mark Wilford, David Windsor and everyone at Avenue Communications, Adrian Bourne, John Hardaker, and all at Haynes Publishing for their commitment to this project. Colleagues on the road, the service of *Autosport* and David Williams's excellent book, *Colin McRae – Rallying's Fast Master*, have provided invaluable information and inspiration. Finally, thanks to my own team for their unwavering support, namely Sue, Natalie and Kate.

Foreword by Colin McRae

Joining Ford at the end of 1998 presented me with the great opportunity and exciting new challenge I was looking for. I felt I needed a change in my career and here were all the ingredients I wanted. It was the right move at the right time.

Malcolm Wilson's M-Sport had taken over the running of Ford's World Rally Championship operation and I knew they had the expertise and ambition required to get the job done. I could also see that Ford Motor Company were making a huge commitment to their whole motorsport programme. It is now plain for everybody to see, not only in rallying but also in Formula One, especially with their acquisition of the Stewart Grand Prix team. It's great that a company like Ford are putting that sort of effort back into motorsport.

The introduction of the Focus marked the start of a new era for Ford and I wanted to be part of that. I was confident this car would set the standard for the future. We were all prepared to endure teething problems for half a season, but it was obvious from our first event, the Monte Carlo Rally, that we had a very competitive car. Even so, it was amazing we were able to win our third and fourth rallies, the Safari and the Rally of Portugal.

Not that it has all been plain sailing. We have had more than our share of

heartache, tension and controversy. In fact, it has been drama at every turn. But then that is the appeal of rallying. It is never predictable, never dull.

The one thing I am certain about is the potential of the Ford Martini team and the Focus. I came to Ford determined to add to my one World Championship, and now I am convinced I shall.

I hope this book gives you an insight into the effort that has been put into our campaign. This is the chance to join us on our roller-coaster ride through the World Rally Championship; to share the thrills and spills, and all the contrasting emotions along the way. Welcome on board.

Introduction

Rallying hasn't always found it easy to catch the attention of the sporting world at large, but on 5 August 1998 it achieved that elusive goal. To be more precise, Ford did. The company signed Colin McRae to lead their World Rally Championship challenge and, with a sense of occasion and style, conducted the formalities on the driver's 30th birthday.

This was no ordinary signing, which of course was why it stirred such global interest. Newspaper headlines screamed of a multimillion pound deal that had catapulted the Scotsman into the pay bracket of the leading Formula One drivers. Some estimates of McRae's retainer were a mite exaggerated but most commentators eventually settled on a figure of about 10 million dollars for the 1999 and 2000 seasons. In rallying, anything approaching this level of remuneration was staggering and the significance was lost on no-one.

Ford meant business, big business, and

The Ford Escort makes its rally debut at San Remo in 1968, driven by Ove Andersson.

the outlay for McRae was a measure of their intent. They were determined to return to the forefront of world rallying, and to accomplish that objective they would need all the best ingredients. McRae was acknowledged as the best, a natural, irresistible talent the popular Press compared with Michael Schumacher in Grand Prix racing. Just as Ferrari brought in the German to head and galvanise their campaign, so Ford looked to McRae.

The initiative sent out the message that Ford were embarking on a new, aggressive, vibrant era. McRae, the youngest ever world rally champion when he took the title in 1995, was a winner and an inspiration, and his prime years were surely still ahead of him. The excited reaction confirmed the message had been duly received. Nobody doubted McRae's ability and single-mindedness, and now there could be no questioning of Ford's commitment.

However, even a driver of McRae's calibre requires the support and weaponry to fulfil his potential. Ford's belief in their new driver was matched by their faith in their World Rally Championship team and the car that would be unleashed at the start of the 1999 season. Martin Whitaker, Ford's Director of European Motorsport, had entrusted Malcolm Wilson and his Cumbria-based M-Sport operation with the company's rallying cause. Wilson's task was to build and develop the car that would beat the world. It was to be the competition version of an instantly acclaimed winner in the market place, the European Car of the Year, the Focus.

Image was important. McRae and Ford's latest creation provided the image of the future. But image was not everything. Substance was necessary to fill the picture. In the showroom and in rallying, that meant results. The goal of the Ford Martini team was the World Rally Championship.

As a production car and a rally car, the Focus had a lot to live up to. On public road and special stage it was replacing a great and much loved champion, the Escort. One of the world's bestselling models had an unparalleled record of success in rallying. In 30 years of drastically changing appearance and technology, the Escort had won 46 world class rallies. Two

London to Mexico 1970 World Cup Rally winners. Left to right: Rauno Aaltonen, Henry Liddon, Gunnar Palm, Hannu Mikkola, Gilbert Staepelaere, Timo Mäkinen.

of those victories were claimed in the RAC Rally by the late Roger Clark. Many more of the sport's greatest drivers had taken the wheel of the Escort.

Ford cars had already built a distinguished reputation in rallying before the appearance of the Escort in 1968. There had been wins at Monte Carlo, on the Safari, the Acropolis and the RAC, and yet nothing could have prepared the sport for the impact of the latest challenger.

The Mark I Escort that made its debut at San Remo, driven by the Swede, Ove Andersson, was a four-speed, rear-wheel drive car with a normally aspirated engine producing about 150bhp. It was essentially white and had back seats. The last factory Escort entered, at the 1998 Network Q Rally of Great Britain, née RAC Rally, had a six-speed sequential gearbox, four-wheel drive, a turbo-charged engine developing 300bhp, sophisticated electronic control systems and advanced safety features. It carried sponsors' colours and logos, and had no back seats.

Roger Clark, twice winner of the RAC Rally.

The Mark I immediately cut a triumphal swathe through rallying, winning the World Championship for Makes in its first two seasons. In 1970 the Mark I won the London to Mexico World Cup Rally – and was subsequently badged Mexico. The original twin-cam was replaced by the RS1600 on world rally events, going on to conquer the East Africa Rally and the Arctic Rally. The Escort's versatility knew no bounds.

The Mark II RS1800 maintained the Escort's remarkable momentum. It delivered a third constructors' title and gave Bjorn Waldegard the Drivers' Championship, ahead of his team-mate, Hannu Mikkola, in 1979. That year the Escort completed a sequence of eight consecutive victories in the RAC. In 1981 Ari Vatanen, also driving an RS1800, became the first privateer to win the World Championship and in all probability he will keep that record to himself forever.

By then the works team was concentrating on developing other models – the four-wheel drive RS200 and Sierra RS Cosworth – but Escorts in various guises and competing in diverse rallies, all around the world, were still winning regularly. A new generation Escort, the RS Cosworth, won five major rallies in 1993: Portugal, Corsica, Acropolis, San Remo and Catalunya. It won twice the following year, and twice again in 1996. Yet another evolution of the Escort, the World Rally Car, built to comply with new competition regulations, claimed two more victories in 1997.

The Escort made a defiant last stand, with podium finishes for Juha Kankkunen and Bruno Thiry, at the 1998 Rally of Great Britain. And yet, even as the Escort bade an emotional farewell, its successor was ready to be put through its paces by Ford's new No. 1 driver.

During the three and a half months after McRae and his co-driver, Nicky Grist, had signed their contracts at Ford's technical development centre in Dunton, Essex, Wilson and his team had completed their building of the Focus, although no-one pretended it had been honed to

Bjorn Waldegard steers the Escort RS1800 to victory on the 1977 East African Rally.

perfection. The team recognised that process would take many more weeks and months to come. They were convinced the Focus would be worthy of Ford's heritage and that McRae would cajole it to the outer limits of its capabilities. No-one, however, anticipated the drama to unfold.

The early period of the McRae–Ford alliance almost defied credibility. It dragged the team into a whirlpool of despair and recrimination, and then propelled them clear in a torrent of celebration and tributes. This is a story of vision and fortitude, ambition and dedication; of torment and relief, confrontation and jubilation. All the elements of sport and human endeavour are fused and magnified in one team's pursuit of a dream.

chapter one

Creation of a winner

In a sense the identification of Ford's new challenger was the easy part. The Focus was designed and heralded as the successor to the bestselling Escort road car. It arrived to its own fanfare and rave reviews. It was European Car of the Year, the car that encapsulated advanced concepts and features in a compact and thoroughly modern body, a car to carry man across the threshold of the new millennium. And what better car to be adapted to the requirements and rarified atmosphere of rallying? So it was that the outline of this neat, nimble creation was handed to those charged with the development of Ford's next winner. This was the start of the more difficult part.

Hard work and heartache had already gone into the laying of the foundations. Malcolm Wilson, a former Ford rally driver, who set up his own team to prepare and run cars from a small workshop in Cumbria, had been contracted to conduct the company's World Championship programme. It is no exaggeration to describe that development as a landmark in the history of Ford Motorsport.

Until 1996 the rallying programme had been the preserve of an in-house team at Boreham. When it was taken out of their control there was, inevitably, much wringing of hands and gnashing of teeth. The internal controversy heaped still more pressure on Wilson, and also on the man who instigated the diversion of the World Rally operation.

Martin Whitaker came to this momentous ruling, supported by like-minded heavyweights within the Ford organisation, from a route through journalism, and Press and Public Relations. He had worked for the RACMSA, and in Formula One specifically for McLaren and the FIA before joining Ford at the beginning of 1995 as Director of Motorsport Communications.

Rallying touches so many people because the cars look like the ones they drive

'It was John Southgate [a company stalwart] who brought me in,' Whitaker said. 'They didn't have anyone looking after the overall communication of motorsport. Ford had almost taken a back seat as far as motorsport competition was concerned and they were looking to try to improve the image of the company within the sport. So I came in and did the job till the summer of '96, when I was given the job of Director of Motorsport for Europe, with responsibility for Formula One and the World Rally Championship.

'The job covers just about everything. The key to it is a liaison role, the central point of contact for all the operations the

Malcolm Wilson on his way to victory in the Escort RS Cosworth, Ulster 1993.

company is running, and therefore being the person who guides and directs the company in whatever direction we choose to take. So, in terms of Formula One, it's very much a case of looking after Ford's interest in the Formula One team, having a very close relationship with the team, particularly Jackie [Stewart], being involved in discussion on drivers' contracts, engine deals, all manner of things, personnel, technical communications, performance, whatever.

'Similarly with the rally programme, it's a case of making sure we are doing things the right way, that we're approaching it in the right manner and communicating that message to the media and the like. Also for touring cars and the rest of the sport. That's more of a delegation role, making sure we're doing what is best, that we're taking the right course of action and direction in terms of Formula Ford, Fiestas, the Puma and Ka rally programmes, and our sports operation in general at Boreham. Now we've become involved in karting, supporting six youngsters and starting them on their motor racing careers with a Ford badge.

'So I'm a Jack of all trades but the single most important thing I hope I've brought to it is better communication within Ford, and brought the motorsport operation back to the attention of senior management. It's a slow process but it does help when you've got people like Jac Nasser [President and CEO of Ford], who's very interested in sport, and Richard Parry-Jones [Group Vice President – Product Development], a former rally man, exerting their influence.'

Bringing rallying, and other forms of motorsport, to the attention of the public is, of course, part of the manufacturers' process for selling cars. And rally cars, unlike Formula One cars, bear a very real resemblance, outwardly at least, to road cars.

'Initially rallying touches so many people because it looks like the car you and I might drive,' Whitaker said. 'From Ford's point of view it's a perfect stage – excuse the pun – on which to demonstrate the performance, driveability and reliability of the product. And – this is where it differs from Formula One – in not such a glamorous world, but in a world where, essentially, you can prove all these factors. If you can win the Safari Rally you've proved pretty conclusively that you've got a strong car. If you can win on tarmac, on the twisting roads of Corsica, you've got a car that proves the right driving dynamics associated with a road car. Also, it's a crucial marketing, communications and advertising tool, as long as you use it correctly.

'I think that in the early nineties Ford had developed a car, in the Escort Cosworth, that was probably the match of anything out there, if not better. The Escort Cosworth is widely believed to be one of the greatest rally cars there's ever been, but it never really achieved its full potential. The reason was, I think, that no-one within the company at the time genuinely believed in the value of the World Rally Championship, or rallying in general. I think there were people, predecessors of mine, like Stuart Turner, who definitely believed in its worth. But there was a vacuum after Turner left, and there wasn't the emphasis or concentration of effort placed on making the Ford Escort a genuine marketing tool, something which had all the right ingredients. It was effectively the last RS product Ford had manufactured so when they ceased production of the Escort Cosworth it was the end of an era, built up on this immense and fantastic tradition, this great heritage of the Escort rally car.

'In the last few years we've resumed the rally programme from a point where they were just about to switch it off to a point where now everybody sees the value in it, they're genuinely interested in it and realise what benefits it can bring to the company. The Focus was designed as a road car and at the beginning I don't think there was any intention of turning it into a rally car. Having said that, it obviously suits being turned into a rally car, which is exactly what Malcolm and his team have done. What I'd like to think is that in the future, just as with the Ford Escort, there will be variants of the Ford Focus which will take the place of the old RS models. They will have styling cues and technical cues that come directly from the rally car, because that's where you really see the benefit of technology transfer from the race track or rally stage to the road.'

However, given all this fabled tradition and heritage, and the existence of a workforce accustomed to the routine, way of life, kudos and perks of the World Rally Championship, the decision to take the operation away from Boreham and place it in the far north-west of England at somewhere called Cockermouth, was bound to be contentious. Whitaker had to be certain of his course. He was.

Martin Whitaker … bold decisions.

'I believe it was vitally important to get Malcolm Wilson involved. You mustn't take away from the team running the works programme what they'd achieved. We were effectively competing with a car that was no longer produced by the company, so we had to get special dispensation to run it as the Escort Rally Car. Boreham was the Mecca of Ford's motorsport programme. This was where everything happened. On the wall at Boreham there's a collage, with images from when it was a Second World War bomber base through to Malcolm Wilson winning the first event the Escort Cosworth ever did, in the early nineties. The next panel will bring it up to the present day, including grand prix cars, GT 40s and all the rest. But to take us through to the future, to run the team as a professional operation, outside the controls that were placed on us at Boreham, it was essential to move it to Cockermouth.

Malcolm Wilson ... determined and professional.

'Why Malcolm? There's something about the personality, the determination of the man. He desperately wants to win. He's also had a long relationship with Ford. Yes, he's been with other manufacturers, such as Austin Rover, Opel and Audi, but he has always had a strong affiliation with Ford. He started rallying, as so many of them do, in an Escort. Now, running a team, he has professional and presentation skills which would be very easy to place in Formula One. You can see that in the equipment he has, his meticulous attention to detail. The car is designed for serviceability. It takes into account the fact you have to change just about everything – the gearbox, the whole rear suspension unit and so on – in a 20-minute service on the Safari.

'And these skills rub off on the people who work for him. He's got a totally dedicated workforce. Having worked at McLaren I can see similarities with Malcolm's team. It's the little things, like making sure the number plates on the rally cars and service vehicles are consecutive. They are S1 to S20. People might ask whether that really matters, but it's the little details that make up the whole. It was quite funny when Malcolm got the plates because the morning after somebody at Ford, who obviously didn't know what was going on, phoned him up and said he thought they should rightly be Ford's. Malcolm told him, in no uncertain terms, he had to get up a lot earlier than that.

'Cumbria was certainly a bridge to cross. We'd tried to move the operation from Boreham to Cockermouth in the summer of '96, not long after I got the job, and it met with a lot of opposition here. There were other dedicated establishments, such as Prodrive, but I felt Malcolm had all the right characteristics and the capability to do the job, even though he didn't yet have special workshops or anything of that nature. I've always relied on this very simple principle, that I don't really mind if you run the car from under the arches at Waterloo station as long as it's successful.

'Of course you're going to need to change the way you approach it, the professionalism and so on. You're going to be using that as a base where you can bring people to corporate activity, hospitality and all that. But as long as we had the dedication of a team of highly motivated individuals to run the programme I wasn't too worried where it was run from. That was what drove me. Having met with a lot of criticism and hit a brick wall within the company to begin with, I realised we had probably been too open about it, and spent too much time talking about it and analysing and strategising. In motorsport you've got to be able to work quickly, make snap decisions and stick to them.

'So Malcolm and I sat down a couple of months later to discuss things. He was still pushing, saying that it was the only way we were going to save the operation. He basically said, "Look Martin, if you're really going to show you've got the bottle, then this is what we've got to do." I suppose I saw the sense and, with Richard Parry-Jones, formed a plan of how we were going to do it. We kept things very much to ourselves, which made it easier to operate. Later that year we were able to announce we were going to move it to Cockermouth. I think it was the turning point in my career. I grew up then. It was a big decision and it wasn't an easy one. We'd taken the core element of Boreham's business away. But we then looked at concentrating different areas of our programme at Boreham and these are growing successfully: the rest of the rallying and other projects such as improving merchandising. We've made the whole thing much more businesslike.

'It left Malcolm with a huge problem because his target then was the Monte Carlo Rally of 1997, with a World Rally Car he didn't have and hadn't prepared. He must have had the most extraordinary December and New Year period. This is what I mean about the dedication of the people he has working there. They didn't see much of Christmas that year.'

Malcolm Wilson drove Fords on 26 World Championship rallies and won the British Championship for the marque in 1994. He was for several years Ford's chief test driver. His insatiable ambition found a new course when he set up his own team, Malcolm Wilson Motorsport. His company's consistent success in international rallying – scoring more than 70 wins – convinced Whitaker he was the man to put in charge of the works operation.

'It all started after Martin got the job of Director of Communications,' Wilson recalled. 'He could see there were areas and aspects that needed change and we

Carlos Sainz ... important role.

talked about what we might do. When Martin was put in the position of Director of Motorsport he thought the simple solution would be for me to go down to Boreham and run the thing there. I didn't think that was the answer and, to be honest, it was probably two years sooner than I'd expected something like this. I'd always planned to stop driving at 40, maybe 43, and get to the position of running a manufacturer team. But by that time our own operation had become very strong, running customers in all parts of the world, with 11 championships in three years. I think third place in Finland, beating a lot of factory teams, proved our ability to do the job.

Guenther Steiner ... ability to motivate.

'Even so, moving it out put Martin under a lot of pressure. People were asking if it could be done from Cumbria, 300 miles from London. I was adamant there was no way I could have gone and done it down the country. OK, we've got an extra half a day on transportation, so you've got to plan to make sure your cars are finished half a day sooner than the cars that are produced in the south of England. I can be at Newcastle Airport as quickly as most people can be at Heathrow and I can park and be in the terminal in two minutes.

'The quality of life for everyone here is also important. We have a fantastic working environment, not an industrial estate, and we have the Lake District National Park here. We don't have other teams nearby, tapping our staff. We don't have the distractions of, say Prodrive, on the M40, with people popping in for a coffee and a chat. I know it happens because I've done it myself. Think of how much productivity they lose because of that. We were able to do what we did with a skeleton staff. When I took on the contract with Ford we had 15 people, and Monte Carlo was seven weeks away.

'Although I didn't want to leave this part of the world I did say at one stage I could do so many days of the week down there. Then I realised it had to be 100 per cent commitment, no division of resources, so one Sunday in September of '96 we sorted it out with Martin. He drove up and we sat him down in front of the log fire, and I said this was the way it had to be done and that I was confident we could do it. Not long after, we were a World Championship team.

'It meant a hell of a job to be ready for the 1997 season but I thought, well, we had Carlos Sainz as our No. 1 driver and we had an Escort I knew we could do a good job with. It was a fantastic car. In fact, it should have won the World Championship for four or five years.'

Sainz, having given Ford one of their two wins in 1996, delivered two more in Wilson's first season of command. The Spaniard would leave before the new era of the Focus, but Whitaker believes he had a significant influence on the company's rallying renaissance.

'Carlos played an incredibly important role, although he probably doesn't realise it,' Whitaker said, 'in the re-establishment of Ford as a major contender in the World Championship. Toyota's loss, getting caught cheating and being thrown out of the Championship, was our gain. All of a sudden Carlos was on the market when Ford's World Championship programme was about to hit rock bottom and probably fall off the scale. We had the opportunity to add to our coffers with the support of Repsol, the state-owned Spanish oil company, who were keen on promoting a Spanish driver, and you can't get a much bigger name in Spain than Carlos Sainz.

'It was pretty difficult to convince Carlos he should join us in the first place but then trying to assure him it was the right move to change the team to Malcolm was a big struggle. But he's a really super guy and a big guy, and he was the first to admit it was the best thing we could have done. We owe an awful lot to Carlos. He's a true professional, as he proved after coming to us probably believing these people were a bunch of no-hopers.'

Malcolm Wilson and his team were moving at the pace of Sainz on a special stage. The little cottage industry would have to develop at the rate of the next car. The old workshop, near his rustic home, would not be able to accommodate their expanding aspirations. Malcolm Wilson Motorsport became the snappier M-Sport. Those two victories in 1997 gave him the muscle to demand still greater responsibility.

Wilson takes up the story: 'The Focus was in the planning [for 1999] but at that stage the idea was that it would be developed by Boreham. I didn't want to start pushing the whole issue but when we'd won a couple of rallies, which people didn't expect in our first year, that gave us a bit more leverage. Eventually I managed to push Martin and we were able to convince Ford we were actually the people to design and develop a completely new car. With no past record.

'Obviously I'd got a lot of ideas that I wanted to put into the Focus. No disrespect, but if it had been done by Ford I'm

MISSION CONTROL CENTRE

An insider's guide to the gadget-packed cockpit that is mission control centre for the Ford Martini World Rally team's Focus car.

1 Instruments
Special LCD display replaces Focus road car panel. Regular display shows engine revs and gear in use, plus a bright light that flashes to indicate best 'change-up' point as revs rise. By turning the black 'Page' knob (bottom right of Central Panel) driver can call-up seven alternative displays or pages - engine, front and centre differentials, front diff only, centre diff only, temperatures (water, oil, brakes, diffs), engine in greater detail, fuel level plus analogues.

2 'Push-to-talk'
Yellow button allows driver to speak with everybody on the team radio network.

3 Gear Selector
High-mounted lever controls six-speed sequential gearbox. Driver pulls lever back to change up, pushes it forward to change down. System permits fast clutchless gear changes, one ratio at a time.

4 Central Panel
This panel features two red adjuster knobs - for brake balance (left) and differential pressure (right). The front and centre diffs can be progressively freed or locked using the two white knobs. Middle row of six 'flick' switches to control heating and lighting. Bottom row has three switches for engine turbo anti-lag system, transmission valves and on stage data logger.

sure they would have incorporated a lot of the old Escort parts into it. We knew it had to be a completely clean sheet of paper. The good thing with the new World Rally Championship regulations is that they enable any manufacturer to build a World Rally Car. You have to build only the 20 kits, not a great number for manufacturers. That's the reason so many people are wanting to come into the Championship.'

Whitaker: 'We knew we had to look beyond the Escort and this was when the idea of the Focus came along. Initially we spoke to our product development people at Dunton, and Richard Parry-Jones and Al Kammerer. Al was the project leader for Focus. They thought the design and development of the new car should be undertaken by Ford, between Dunton and Boreham. But Malcolm was now in a

much greater position of strength to call the shots and he said, "No, I'm going to build a completely new design and development team and we'll do the job." We had numerous meetings, with both Richard and Al, and we decided to bite the bullet and give him the opportunity to do it.'

For all Wilson's faith in Cumbria, he could not summon the facility for this task within the time-scale and even he had to acknowledge a more central location would be the practical solution. The search for suitable premises to create the Focus World Rally Car led them to industrial units at Millbrook, Bedfordshire. Wilson: 'The big problem was the security aspect because the road car wasn't even launched to the public. There were all sorts of confidentiality things we had to sign. You could take a building somewhere in the Midlands and spend an awful lot on security, so we looked at Millbrook and MIRA. We decided on Millbrook: total security, no windows, test track on site. It really did fit the bill. We moved in there in February '98.'

Whitaker: 'He needed to be in the centre of the country, within a stone's throw of his suppliers. From the first day I went there with Malcolm and saw this shell of a building, which I think was squeezed between Rolls-Royce and a Korean operation, in the back end of Millbrook workshops, it was the most remarkable experience to watch the whole thing develop and see them very diligently working away at producing this car. The facilities and the high degree of secrecy made it a logical place and it all paid off because not a single person saw a photograph of the car until it was launched.'

They had a no compromise approach to getting the best performance

Wilson had raised a few more eyebrows with his choice of Project Leader. Guenther Steiner was an experienced rallying team player from northern Italy but had no track record for a task such as this. He had worked for the distinguished Jolly Club motorsport operation, which achieved three Italian Rally Championship successes with the Escort Cosworth. He moved to Britain to join Prodrive in 1996. Now he was charged with co-ordinating all aspects of the construction, testing and development of the Focus.

Wilson: 'Guenther's not a qualified engineer, he's just a guy who's got a great ability to motivate people and get the job done. He oversees the team of designers. He's got a wealth of experience and, like myself, an understanding of what's needed from the car. So he is able to look at what the designers are doing and say, "This is not strong enough for Kenya," because he's been out in the bush. Or he might say, "Come on, this is over the top for asphalt," because he knows what it's all about.

'We got started on the job but we had no car, so we had to get linked into the Ford mainstream computer to get all the info and did it all in record time. It's very difficult initially when you've not got a car to put your hands on because you're wondering if you could just do this or that. Obviously the designers and engineers could work off drawings, but until I had the hardware I found it hard to visualise.'

There were, however, guiding principles which Wilson and his team were never to lose sight of. They adopted a 'no compromise' approach to achieving the best possible performance and were committed to 'putting the weight where we want it', that is low down and within the wheelbase to create an agile but more driveable car. Also, as Martin Whitaker has explained, serviceability was paramount. It would have the shape and general appearance of the road car, but in many ways be a totally different car, created and developed to beat the best rally cars in the world.

THE FORD FOCUS RALLY CAR

- Rally car design starts with a clean sheet of paper.
- Design builds on attributes of Ford Focus road car.
- Zetec E engine with bespoke turbocharger optimised for fast response.
- Longitudinal six-speed sequential gearbox for optimum weight distribution.
- Four-wheel drive with three active differentials. Rear differential is particularly compact for increased ground clearance.
- Longest wheelbase in class provides stability and allows key components to be located in the middle of the car. For example:
- Fuel tank mounted amidships for optimum weight distribution – 52:48 weight distribution becomes 50:50 with downforce from the rear wing at speed.
- Engine moved back 20mm and tilted backwards at an angle of 25°.

- Long travel strut suspension with new low friction wheel bearings.
- 30 per cent stiffer shell than Ford Escort World Rally Car.
- Extensive use of lightweight materials, e.g. titanium pedals, steering racks and hubs.

The conception and production of an all-new rally car usually takes about 18 months. The Ford Focus World Rally Car was running 317 days after the programme had been sanctioned. Fifty-three days later it made its competitive debut at the Monte Carlo Rally. This is the diary of the Focus's creation:

December 1997

- Ford management decides that the design and development of the new Ford Focus World Rally Car should be undertaken by Cumbria based M-Sport.
- M-Sport begins investigating new premises in the Midlands to be located more in the heart of the world's motorsport industry, closer to major suppliers and industry testing facilities.
- First meetings held with Ford in Cologne during the Christmas 'break'. M-Sport staff view the glass-fibre mock-up of the proposed Focus World Rally Car and collect detailed information. Broad outlines of exterior shape of car already decided by Ford.

January 1998

- Search for suitable premises continues. Industrial units at Millbrook in Bedfordshire selected because of central location, immediate availability, testing facilities on the doorstep and

Driver's eye view in the Ford Focus WRC.

excellent security to ensure the high level of confidentiality required by Ford.

- Advertising for and interviewing of new staff begins.

February 1998

- The embryonic M-Sport Focus team moves to Millbrook. Computer systems established and brought on-line with Ford's Small and Medium Vehicle Centre at Dunton and Cologne for instant information transfer. Road car data downloaded to facilitate start of design work on the rally car.
- Two prototype bodyshells – body-in-white shells – delivered to Millbrook. First new designer starts work on 14th; major recruitment push during rest of month.
- Contracts signed with engine and gearbox manufacturers, Mountune and XTrac.

March 1998

- Detailed design work in full swing from beginning of month. Conclusion of the build-up period acquiring data, fitting out the Millbrook facility and putting together the team of people to work on the project.

April 1998

- Design work continues. Starting with nothing proves to be an advantage and a disadvantage. Re-inventing everything, the design team proceeds cautiously to avoid 'blind alleys' on particular components.

May 1998

- Roll cage design and stress analysis completed mid-month. Dummy cage fitted to mock-up shell. Tooling designed and ordered for the major body panels with long lead times.

June 1998

- Suspension design finalised and components ordered.

The hot seats in the Ford Focus WRC.

Mc RAE
sparco
sparco
Sabelt
Sabelt
sparco

July 1998
- First sets of suspension components received at Millbrook.

August 1998
- First complete World Rally Car bodyshell – with full roll cage and modified wheel arches – completed. Final assembly of first Focus rally car gets underway.
- M-Sport Focus team now totals 15 staff working alongside several contractors' personnel.

September 1998
- First engine delivered by Mountune at beginning of month.
- Prototype Focus World Rally Car makes world debut at Paris Show on 29th.

October 1998
- First gearbox delivered on the 12th.

Engine installation finalised, and engine fired up for the first time in car on the 21st. Car takes to the test track for the first time on the 22nd – Malcolm Wilson at the wheel. Engine mapping completed.

November 1998
- Testing goes to schedule, with Focus WRC running on track at least four days in every seven. Performance and reliability of mechanical parts is excellent. Additional M-Sport staff from Cumbria on site to assist with build programme.
- Homologation papers completed and submitted to the FIA on the 15th.
- Ford Focus World Rally Car presented to the media on the 25th.

FORD FOCUS WORLD RALLY CAR
Technical Specification

Engine: Ford 2.0 L Zetec E 4-cylinder, 16-valve, 2-litre.

The Ford Focus WRC's power house.

Electronic Ford engine management system. Garrett turbocharger (with FIA required 34mm restrictor). Catalytic converter.
Electronics: Full chassis and engine data acquisition for on-event diagnostics and performance development.
Intercooler: Air/air intercooler with external water spray.
Power: 300bhp at 6,500rpm.
Torque: 550Nm at 4,000rpm.
Fuel Tank: 100-litre capacity/located centrally.
Drive system: Permanent 4-wheel drive with M-Sport designed and manufactured active front, centre and mechanical rear differentials. Electronic differential control units.
Transmission: Ford/XTrac 240 6-speed sequential gearbox.
Suspension: *Front:* Macpherson struts with adjustable dampers. Fully adjustable links. *Rear:* Macpherson struts with adjustable dampers and adjustable links.
Steering: Power-assisted high-ratio (12:1) rack and pinion. 1.5 turns lock to lock.
Brakes: *Asphalt:* 380mm (front)/315mm (rear) ventilated discs with 8-pot calipers (front)/4-pot calipers (rear). *Gravel:* 300mm ventilated discs, 4-pot calipers (front & rear).
Wheels: *Asphalt:* 18in diameter x 8in wide. *Gravel:* 15in diameter x 7in wide. *Snow:* 16in diameter x 5in wide.
Overall length: 4,152mm
Wheelbase: 2,615mm
Overall width: 1,770mm
Weight: 1,230kg
Overall height: 1,420mm

Ford World Rally Team Partners

Lubricants: Valvoline
Tyres: Michelin
Wheels: OZ
Brakes: Brembo
Racewear: Sparco

Constructing a World Rally Car to such a stringent time-scale challenges a team's ingenuity and powers of improvisation. M-Sport came up with an unlikely means of evaluating their progress one weekend late in September. Guenther Steiner takes up the story:

'We arrived at the stage where the suspension and everything else on the car was finished. It even had an engine in. But there was no transmission as it was a completely new concept. It was supposed to arrive at the end of August, then the

First picture of the Focus WRC, minus transmission, at Millbrook.

end of September, and when we didn't have it then we said we couldn't wait another three weeks standing around. We had major work to do. Our schedule for Monte Carlo was tight and we had to check the parts because the lead times for items such as the uprights were so long.

'We were talking about what we might do and someone suggested towing the car around. It started as a joke and we all laughed, but the more we thought about it the more it seemed not such a crazy idea after all. This might not be our idea of how to build a rally car but we just needed to find out if the uprights would stay together, if something would crack, if the car was basically sound.

'At Millbrook they have test facilities for all kind of conditions, including a demanding surface of stones, very hard on the suspension. It is not unlike the Acropolis. Car manufacturers use it for their durability tests. So we decided to give it a try, towing the car with my Scorpio. We had to put weight in the car to make up for the missing gearbox and all the other stuff, and of course we needed drivers. That was no problem. We had plenty of volunteers among the boys. It was a bit of fun for them as well as serious work.

A novel test run for the almost completed Focus WRC – and the Scorpio.

'We did it on a weekend, when it was quiet. We didn't really want people seeing what we were doing because it was a strange approach. So we took it out one Saturday and towed it around for eight hours. We had to keep changing the driver in the rally car because it was so difficult to steer. We didn't travel at high speeds, just enough to check the suspension and the rest of the car. The Scorpio was struggling at the end. It is not made to be a rally car but it proved itself to be a good car, also.

'Almost everything was fine on the rally car but we did find one little problem with the uprights. We made a design change straightaway and integrated it into the uprights for Monte Carlo, so it was a worthwhile exercise. I have never heard of people using this technique before, but not a lot of people would tell you if they did. When you are in situations like these you have to use your imagination.'

Driving Ford rally cars 'straight from the box' was no new experience for Wilson. He had been the first to drive a range of RS and Cosworth challengers over the years. This, though, was different. This was his baby, and when he took the Focus out on to the test track on 22 October 1998, he was the consummate doting parent.

'I'd a history of being the first person to

drive a new car for Ford, so I kept up the tradition. As with all new cars you know there's no point in taking risks and damaging it, so in one sense it's always a disappointment. But obviously there was a different feeling about this one. The whole thing had built up and built up till finally you get in the car. And when I got in this car I could tell there was more potential with it than anything else I'd driven.

'Usually you think, "Oh, there's a big flat spot there, it runs out of breath there." When I got into this it was, "Gosh, yeah, engine feels good right away, it's responsive. Gear linkage, that's not quite right, but the speed of the change is good." I got out of it feeling there wasn't mountains of work still to be done. That was the relief for me because Monte Carlo was two and half months away. OK, there was work to be done, but not so many things to do again. That was down to getting the right people involved, people with good understanding of rallying and what was required. It gave us a great platform. Our target was the Championship in 2000 and I felt confident we could achieve that.'

Wilson scoured the north for new premises to house his team and nurture his dreams. The workforce was up to 87 by the middle of 1999 and is due to num-

Ford President Jac Nasser introduces the Ford Focus WRC at the Paris Show.

ber 150 by the end of 2000. He settled for a place just the other side of Cockermouth, and the entire operation is scheduled to move in at the end of 1999. To call it a factory is to call the Focus World Rally Car a nice little runner. Dovenby Hall is a listed building. It was once a mental institution.

'Yes, it helps to be a lunatic at this job,' Wilson cheerfully obliged. 'It will be magnificent. It's such a beautiful big old building, with lots of great features. We've built all the workshop area inside the confines of the original walled grounds and we've had the sheet roof done in a similar colour to the original tiles, so it doesn't look out of place. And it is massive. It's on a site of 115 acres of lovely rolling parkland and trees. Outside the offices there's a 400-year-old oak.'

He's bitten some serious bullets, especially with the design of the new car

There is, of course, a price to be paid for all this ambition. Ford invest around 30 million dollars a year in the World Rally Championship programme and entrust Wilson with the budget.

Whitaker said: 'Ford effectively has 100 per cent ownership of the World Championship team and we delegate the responsibility for running the programme to Malcolm, just as we do the Grand Prix programme to Jackie Stewart. Malcolm is the driving force, he's the business manager, he's the director of the operation. He's never come to us for more money. He runs a tight ship, he spends his money wisely. He understands what it takes to do this business, he understands what it's going to cost to win. He's bitten some serious bullets, particularly with the design of the new car, and he's signed some cheques that I think would have made a number of people gulp. But he knew this was what he had to do.

'It was very obvious he needed a new factory because the premises he had weren't going to be the place for the future of Ford's World Championship operation. While tending to everything else, Malcolm visited 39 or 40 sites in the north-west and north-east of England before deciding where he wanted to put his new factory. We'd created a success, we'd created a talking point, we'd created something which the company realised was a jewel in the making.'

chapter two

Recruiting a winner

Motorsport enthusiasts will forever debate the relative values of car and driver in competition, and there is, of course, no definitive equation. However, it is indisputable that the performance of even the best car will be enhanced in the hands of the better drivers. Malcolm Wilson, Martin Whitaker and the rest of the hierarchy at Ford were mindful of that basic rationale when they plotted the creation of the Focus and their assault on the World Rally Championship.

'I'd always believed,' Whitaker said, 'that you could build the best car in the world, but that if you didn't have one of the best drivers in the world driving it then you'd probably be wasting your time. We knew we needed a name, we needed somebody who could really pedal this car.'

The much admired Carlos Sainz, twice world champion, had returned to his spiritual home, Toyota, in 1998. The last season of the Escort was piloted by Sainz's nemesis, Juha Kankkunen of Finland, and Belgium's Bruno Thiry. Kankkunen, with four world titles and 21 rally wins to his credit, had pedigree and Thiry, it was widely held, had unfulfilled talent. But the new era demanded the new man, the new driving force; someone to take the Focus by the scruff of the neck, someone to convince the world Ford were serious about their rallying again. The identikit would fit only one driver.

'Colin McRae was the man perfectly suited to the job,' Whitaker said emphatically. That conviction was shared by Wilson: 'Martin and I had been discussing Colin as far back as '97. We felt he was the driver we had to have. You just had to look at what he'd done for Subaru, especially Subaru UK. And an important factor as far as I was concerned, with a brand new car, was to have somebody as aggressive and determined as Colin driving the car. Because he's the one who can find the weak spots sooner than anybody else.

Having Colin has cut the learning process by at least six months

'We didn't want a driver who was easy on the car. For instance, Juha was fantastic in a car. He'd do a rally, you'd bring the car back, wash it and you could have gone straight out again and done another rally. Now that's great if you're into an easy life, and he's a great guy to have on board a World Championship team, but that was not what we needed with this car. We needed to find the limits of everything as soon as possible. By having Colin I believe you cut your learning process by at least six months.

'So we were looking at it from two

Juha Kankkunen gets to grips with typically Swedish conditions in 1998, the last World Championship campaign of the works Ford Escort.

angles. Firstly, Colin is the best. We have no doubt about that. He's the fastest driver in the World Championship. But he was also right for us at the time to get the car sorted for 2000, which was our target for the Championship. There were a lot of things he could address in '99 to put him in a strong position for the following year.

'He's very good with feedback. Like myself, he's been with cars and involved in competition all his life, even if it was bikes to begin with. He's got a feeling for it. He can see the little things instantly. Again, that helps our engineers and designers. They're not wasting time and effort. They're able to get on with it.

'People say Colin seems shy and quiet, but I can tell you, he's not shy when it's anything to do with the car. He just tells you. He's straight to the point. That's

what we need. It can be hard for a lot of the boys and engineers. Sometimes they get a kicking from him. But then it's my job to come in and say, "Look boys, hang on, you've got to understand that we've got the best driver in the world here. We've got to sort it this year and next year hopefully we'll win the Championship."'

Ford's initial approach for the Scotsman was rebuffed but in the summer of 1998 he, too, was ready for a new challenge. A two-year contract worth 10 million dollars not only put him into the Formula One pay bracket but also confirmed the company's commitment to the World Rally Championship programme.

Whitaker: 'We knew that Colin had extremely strong links with Subaru, having been there eight years and enjoyed phenomenal success. But, as with anything else, what you don't ask for in life you don't get, and we figured it was important to approach him and see what the chances were. Somewhat surprisingly, we found there was a big interest, and eventually we were able to sign him. Not wishing to be derogatory to either Juha Kankkunen or Bruno Thiry, but I do feel that had we got Colin the year before, which we really wanted to do, and put him in the Escort, I think he'd have won the Championship. It would have been a great swansong for the Escort WRC and it's a crying shame it won only a handful of events.

'Colin still needed some convincing that Malcolm could really do the job, and don't forget it was a bold decision by Colin. People say it was based on the fact we paid him a lot of money, but that's not the case at all. These drivers want to win. Maybe five or six years down the road, as Colin's getting older and thinking about the day when he might be hanging up his driving gloves, he might consider the money first. But at the position he is in his life and his career, the most important thing to him was to continue winning and having the right equipment. So it was a big gamble from his point of view to come with Ford, to a completely unproven, untested, untried product. When he signed the car wasn't on four wheels, so again that demonstrated the persuasive powers of Malcolm Wilson.

'You could argue we would have been happy to have continued right through with Carlos Sainz. He has got just as good a reputation and there's a case for saying he is a safer option than Colin. But we knew Carlos was sorely tempted by Toyota when they were allowed back in the Championship. That was his home. He wanted to be comforted by a nice cosy sofa in front of a warm fire, and that was what Toyota was to him. He'd always been desperate to go back.

'You weigh it all up. Yes, Colin probably needs some rough edges smoothing off, but what would you rather have, an aggressive driver who's going to win rallies for you, which in a sense Ford's motorsport operation had forgotten how to, or somebody who is going to abide by our old competition strategy of competing to compete rather than competing to win? We'd rather have somebody who was going to go out there and flog the car to death, and win.

Malcolm Wilson and Martin Whitaker clasp their hands on Colin McRae and Nicky Grist at last.

'Image is important but it's horses for courses. The importance of Colin is his reputation as an aggressive, flamboyant competitor and a winner. Ultimately that's what you want as a company. Because that's what's going to affect your performance, that's what's hopefully going to improve your revenue in terms of merchandising sales and going to increase the visibility of your product because he's going to be winning with it. If he says something out of line you've got to learn to take it and you've also got to be tough enough to sit down with him and say, "Right Colin, you've said it now, but that's the last time we want to hear you say that."

'We wanted to get emotion back into what we were doing and, again, Colin fits in with this general strategy. We have adverts with the car leaping in the air, and there's emotion there. And the advert showing a young, dreaming Colin and the grown-up, rally star Colin had tremendous response. There's feeling and emotion in that commercial. That's what we want at Ford.'

Whitaker would have to deal with the emotional, outspoken McRae early in the 1999 season, as we shall discover, but on 5 August 1998, at Ford's technical development centre in Dunton, Essex, not a ripple or frown was in evidence. It was Colin McRae's 30th birthday – reason enough to be sanguine. But this was also the occasion of his formal commitment to Ford. The world champion driver of 1995, and runner-up in '96 and '97 and his co-driver, Nicky Grist, signed two-year contracts.

'The move to Ford provides me with a unique and fresh challenge,' McRae's official statement began. 'I will be playing a major role in the development of an all-new World Rally Car. At the same time, Ford's total commitment to winning the World Championship means that my own title-winning ambitions do not have to be put on hold while the new car is developed. The rally car is as radical as the road car and it is clear that I will be driving not just one of the fastest competition cars in the world but one which is also undoubtedly the best looking.'

The smiling harmony was on display again at the Paris Motor Show a few weeks later, when the Focus World Rally Car – or

Family affair … Colin McRae with mother Margaret, father Jimmy and brother Alister, 1991.

at least a fairly convincing mock-up – was unveiled. Ford President Jac Nasser declared: 'Colin McRae's signing is a real vote of confidence in Ford's ability to win at the highest level of motorsport. His immense natural talent, together with the new levels of reliability and performance set by the Ford Focus rally car, will make the Ford team very hard to beat in 1999.'

It is perhaps too glib to say McRae was born to rally, but when your father is five times British champion there has to be something in the genes. McRae senior never actively coaxed or cajoled the first of his three sons along his tyre tracks. It simply happened, just as naturally as bleak winter follows undependable summer in their native Lanark. Colin cut his competitive teeth on motorbikes, just as his father had, in scrambling and trials, graduating to four wheels in 1986. The momentum was unstoppable.

That Motu Road performance secured him a place in rallying folklore

Motorsport bound the family. Colin's brothers, Alister and Stuart, joined the regular weekend treks to the forests, and their mother, Margaret, tended her menfolk as wives and mothers do. Stuart eventually opted for a career in catering but Alister pursued the rallying course and the McRae clan became the scourge of domestic competitions. Colin, Alister and Jimmy were first, second and fourth on the 1992 Scottish Rally. They etched the family name in the history books when all three competed in the 1997 RAC Rally.

However, for all the success of Jimmy and the potential of Alister, it was Colin who made McRae synonymous with the best and most exciting in world rallying. His bravado gave him grief and brought him into conflict with authority, both within his team and ruling bodies, but his was a rare and irresistible talent. In sport true greatness is measured not only in medals but also by the impact on the senses. Colin McRae has the power to bring an impassive gallery to life, to confound even the most seasoned and sceptical observer. As we shall hear again and again, he is recognised as the rallying equivalent of Ayrton Senna and Michael Schumacher.

Less than a year after making his rallying debut in a Talbot Sunbeam, he was competing in a World Rally Championship event. He was 18 years old. McRae finished 36th on the 1987 Swedish Rally, driving a Vauxhall Nova, the car with which he won his class in that year's British Championship. He had more class success with the Peugeot Junior team in 1988 and was runner-up in the British Championship the following year driving a Ford Sierra Cosworth with the RED team.

In 1991 he began his eight-year association with the Banbury-based Subaru team, Prodrive boss David Richards relenting after being badgered by McRae Snr. Colin was British champion in his first season, winning four of the six events. The following year he defended his title with outrageous ease, winning all six rounds. At last Britain had another world-class driver, a genuine successor to Roger Clark. He confirmed as much with victory in the 1993 Rally of New Zealand, becoming the first Briton to win a round of the World Championship since Clark's triumph at the 1976 RAC Rally.

In the process, he tamed one of the most awesome stages in world rallying, the tight, twisting, slippery Motu Road. McRae beat some of the finest drivers in the business by three-quarters of a minute and more. That extraordinary performance gave him command of the event and secured a place in rallying lore.

The following year McRae repeated his achievement in New Zealand and then, to unconfined British pride and joy, demolished all comers to win the RAC. That result buoyed his confidence after an erratic season, removed the tension within the team, and propelled him into his successful Championship campaign of 1995. Aided, admittedly, by an injury to Sainz, he surged from behind and sealed the title with another stirring victory on his home event. The youngest ever Scottish champion, the youngest ever winner of a British international rally, and the youngest ever British champion was now, at the age of 27, the youngest ever world champion.

McRae was runner-up in 1996, after more friction within the Subaru camp, and again in 1997, despite winning five rallies, more than any other driver. He had, however, led Subaru to a third consecutive Manufacturers' Championship. Driver and team had endured anguish, much of it very public, along the way, but the results had justified 'the chance' taken by Richards back in 1991. McRae's achievements were officially recognised by the nation in 1996 with the award of an MBE.

If there remained those who were reluctant to accept the Scotsman had left behind his 'McCrash' days, few could question his innate skill and versatility. He had proved his pace on tarmac, gravel, the rugged tracks of the Safari and the varied conditions of the RAC, and had consistently seen off the opposition in the Asia-Pacific series. In 1998 he won in Portugal, Corsica and Greece, but mechanical problems elsewhere undermined his Championship aspirations and he finished third.

He parted company with Subaru after his home rally and a few days later was flexing the muscles of the newly-built Ford Focus. Soon joining him was his navigator of the previous two years, Nicky Grist, regarded as one of the world's outstanding exponents of the craft. Grist's previous partners included Kankkunen, Armin Schwarz and an Englishman called Malcolm Wilson.

Grist, born in Abergavenny, Wales, on 1 November 1961, brought not only experience and a proven track record, but also personality and an infectious enthusiasm.

He talks and plays a good game. He is meticulous in his preparation, indefatigable in his commitment to the job. If heads are down, Grist is as likely as anyone to lift them. Out of the car he is a constantly active figure, a small whir of perpetual motion: checking this, reassessing that. McRae acknowledges his cause could not be in better guiding hands.

The Welshman took to the rallying trail in 1982, when he was still seemingly bent on a more sedate, and considerably less perilous, sporting life in golf. Against

Sweden's Thomas Rådström, brought in as McRae's No. 2 to focus on the gravel rallies.

earnest advice back at the 19th, he opted for the dubious privilege of sitting next to the crazed breed called rally drivers and there, amazingly for an otherwise apparently bright and well-adjusted adult, he has stayed.

Ford must accept some responsibility, providing Grist with his first professional contract for the World Rally Championship in 1990. He partnered Wilson in the Sierra Cosworth on three tarmac events of the 1991 Championship. They had a best place of fifth in Corsica. In 1992 Grist was introduced to the daunting Safari, co-driving for Mikael Ericsson. The following year he was summoned to join Kankkunen just days before the Rally of Argentina and they won the event.

They teamed up again for the final three rallies of that season, with resounding success. They won in Australia, were third in Spain and defied particularly hostile conditions on the RAC Rally to round off their Championship triumph with another victory. The winning combination remained intact for the 1994 and 1995 campaigns. In 1994 they won in Portugal and were second on the Monte Carlo, New Zealand and RAC Rallies. They scored consistently the following season but this time they were to miss the RAC. Toyota were excluded from the Championship for a year after using an illegal turbocharger restrictor. Kankkunen and Grist were restricted to three outings in 1996, producing familiar form to take second place in Finland.

It proved their last significant result together. At the end of the year Grist was offered the chance to join the Subaru team as co-driver to McRae. The Scotsman's long-time partnership with Derek Ringer had run its course. Grist measured up the requirements and he embarked on the next challenge of his career. The new pairing rattled up five wins in their first season, but with insufficient back-up results they were denied the world title by a point. Three more victories in 1998 gave them third place in the final standings.

Simon Jean-Joseph, from Martinique, who was to concentrate on the asphalt duties.

By then Grist, like McRae, had signed a two-year deal with Ford and turned his attention to the Focus programme. He would not, however, find his old running mate, Kankkunen, there to welcome him. The Finn had chosen to move in the opposite direction, effectively changing places with McRae. It had been supposed Kankkunen would stay and provide the steady, reliable foil to McRae's exuberance. Wilson was satisfied he had agreed a deal in principle with Kankkunen but the hype that accompanied McRae's signing – and speculation about his salary – palpably changed the landscape. Kankkunen wanted more money, and sought the security of a two-year contract. Wilson felt he could not comply and the Finn made for Banbury to take the vacant seat at Subaru.

'On the face of it McRae and Kankkunen would have been a good pairing,' Wilson conceded. 'But when you consider Juha's indifferent ability on asphalt I think we would still have been looking to a three- or four-driver line-up. The way rallying is going, the cost of it and everything, we would always have wanted to bring on a youngster as well. I can't deny, though, that Colin and Juha would have been an ideal combination. I don't know how Juha would have coped with some of the things on the new car and in any case I wouldn't have been prepared to make a commitment for the year 2000.

'I could understand Juha's attitude over the money. Colin's figure was bandied about, so he obviously felt he was worth more than he was getting. It was still a very handsome salary and I'm absolutely sure he would have been more than happy with it. We couldn't agree but it was amicable enough at the end and we're still friends. In fact, he bought a car from us. So with Juha gone we said, "OK, let's look at the thing differently." It had always been the plan to develop the car and put all the effort behind Colin, so we decided to look to the future and try a few people. That would also help keep a bit of the pressure off him.'

Wilson decided to try Sweden's Thomas Rådström and Simon Jean-Joseph, from Martinique. Rådström would undertake the bulk of the Championship programme, essentially the gravel events, as McRae's No. 2, and Jean-Joseph, more comfortable on tarmac, would be brought in for Monte Carlo, Catalunya, Corsica and San Remo. The final member of the squad would be a Norwegian, Petter Solberg.

Petter Solberg, the young Norwegian appointed to the squad for a five-year programme.

Since Rådström is two and a half years older than McRae he scarcely qualifies as a youngster, but in World Championship terms he was relatively inexperienced, with only 19 events and no wins to his name when Ford hired him. However, being Scandinavian he had almost instinctively taken to the sport. Just three days after getting his driving licence, the 18-year-old entered his first rally at the wheel of his mother's Volvo 140. He developed all-round skills by competing on snow and ice rallies in winter and in rallycross in the summer. In 1987 he won the Nordic Rallycross Championship.

The following year he joined the Swedish Junior Rally Team, driving an Audi Quattro, and in 1989 finished second in the Swedish Junior Championship. He switched to Toyota and in 1991 went one better in the Swedish Junior Championship. He graduated from a Group N Celica to Group A and finished third in the 1993 Swedish Championship. His first major victory came in the 1994 Swedish Rally, although it did not qualify as a full World Championship round under FIA's rotation system. He rounded off the year with another third place in the national championship and the Nordic Rally Championship title.

Signing three drivers to partner Colin laid a solid platform for the future

His reward was elevation to the professional ranks in 1995. He joined Toyota Team Sweden to drive not only in the national championship but also in selected World Championship events. He reciprocated with third place in the Swedish Rally, his best World Championship result, and victory on the South Swedish Rally assured him another national third place. In 1996 he won the national title and achieved a creditable sixth place in Finland's 1000 Lakes Rally.

Rådström earned more World Championship points with fifth place on the 1997 Acropolis Rally. He was allowed to spread his wings with his most extensive World Championship programme to date in 1998, representing Toyota Team Sweden in the FIA Teams Cup. He was nominated as an official Toyota driver for the Swedish Rally and led the event until he crashed on the second day. Sixth place in Finland contributed to another productive season and the case for his call-up by Ford. He signed a one-year contract with a view to driving the Focus in Sweden, Kenya, Portugal, Argentina, Greece, New Zealand, Finland, Australia and Great Britain.

'I learned much about the Championship by competing in the FIA Teams Cup and to link up with the Ford Focus represents a major step for me,' Rådström said. 'It can only help me and the team by having someone as experienced as Colin McRae as my team-mate.'

If Sweden is one of the first countries you might explore for rallying talent then Martinique is surely one of the last. But it was there, in his Caribbean homeland, that Jean-Joseph developed his driving talent to the extent that he caught the attention of the European establishment. He won 25 rallies in Martinique and Guadeloupe between 1990 and 1997, and raised his international stock with impressive performances in France. He was running in the top ten on his first World Championship event, the Tour of Corsica, before he was forced to retire with mechanical problems. After a break from the French Championship he returned in 1997 and his consistent success in 1998 earned him his place in the Ford squad.

Unsurprisingly, he had become a major celebrity back home. He was named Martinique's Sportsman of the Year in 1993, and the island's Personality of the Year for 1996 and 1997. He is only 10 months younger than McRae, but his limited World Championship opportunities rendered him a virtual novice and Wilson had a hunch he possessed largely untapped potential.

'I look at this opportunity in the long term,' Jean-Joseph said. 'My initial aim is to gather experience of the Ford Focus in a competitive environment and to learn more about the rallies themselves.'

The choice of Solberg was a definite punt into the future. Born on 18 November 1974, the Norwegian didn't make his rally debut until 1996. However, like McRae he came from a motorsport family and like Rådström he was competing within days of qualifying for his driving licence. His father, Terje, and mother, Tove, took part in autocross and rallying events. Petter entered the arena in autocross and widened his horizons on the rallycross track and on hillclimbs. He had a privately-entered Mark II Ford Escort. He was second in both the rallycross and hillclimb championships of Norway in 1994.

Solberg switched to a Volvo 240 in the Supernational class of 1995 and attracted even more attention. He won the Norwegian Championship in both rallycross and hillclimbing and emulated the feat the following year. Flushed with success he launched his rallying career. He drove his elder brother Henning's Toyota Celica in Norway's Hedmarksrally – and destroyed the vehicle in a big accident. To compound his discomfiture, the incident was captured for national television by the on-board cameras.

Undeterred, he drove a Group A Toyota Celica in the Norwegian Rally Championship and hillclimb series of 1997. Victory on the penultimate rally helped him to fifth in the championship and he took the hillclimb title for four-wheel drive Group A cars. In 1998 he concentrated his efforts on rallying and the commitment paid dividends. Driving a Toyota GT4 he became the Norwegian champion after winning four of the six rounds. He won a round of the Swedish Championship, and was second on the South Swedish Rally and the Rally of Lebanon. Victories on several smaller rallies completed the persuasive portfolio he presented to Wilson.

'Petter first came to my notice in the Middle East, competing on the Lebanon Rally. He was only a boy, he'd never done an asphalt rally before. He was driving a Toyota, and he was actually beating our latest spec Escort. Then, with no contact at all, he sent me a video of him in action. I watched it and some of his driving is pretty committed stuff. So I thought we'd take a closer look. We got Simon over, we got Petter over and we brought in Stuart Egglestone, because we needed the reference, and we went to one of the forest stages we use for testing, in Cumbria, to do an analysis of them.

'We got the engineers there as well, did things with the car, and said, "Right, go and drive it, and give us your feedback." Fred Gallagher [the team's No. 2 co-dri-

Malcolm Wilson puts Fred Gallagher on the case.

Phil Mills. His was a dual role – assistant to the team's co-ordination manager, John Millington, and co-driver to Petter Solberg.

ver] sat with them, seeing how good they were at making the pace notes. I thought everything about Petter was right. The kid was totally committed, he's got flair, a good personality, and we gave him a five-year programme: a few rallies in the first year and, all being well, ten in the second year.

'The original idea was for him to drive the Escort on four events. That was a commercial decision. But then we got the opportunity to put him in the Focus and we took it. That meant we could start to run things on his car that we'd not been running on the factory car and could get more feedback. It took longer than I would have liked to get into that position, because of the time required to build the Focus and the problems we had, but at last we were able to think about incorporating into his car some of the things we'd maybe use in 2000.'

Whitaker heartily approves of Solberg's appointment. 'Petter, I think, is a star of the future,' he said. 'They call him Hollywood and it's not difficult to see why. He's got the looks, he's got the personality and, crucially, he's got the driving ability as well. He's got everything.'

A team doesn't have everything without its full complement of co-drivers. Gallagher is one of the most experienced, respected and popular navigators in the business. The Ulsterman, born in 1952, began his rallying career when McRae was a toddler. He partnered Tony Pond and the late Henri Toivonen, then had eight successful years with Toyota, alongside Kankkunen and Bjorn Waldegard. He had three victories on the Safari before surviving a horrific incident on the Kenyan event in 1992. The Toyota caught fire during a refuelling at a service area and Gallagher was pulled from the blaze by Waldegard.

Gallagher had taken a liking to rally raids and in 1993 joined Citroën. Since then he has helped Timo Salonen and Ari Vatanen surmount a variety of desert and cross-country challenges. The RAC recognised his wealth of knowledge when in 1994 they appointed him Clerk of the Course for their World Championship event.

Solberg's inclusion in the squad necessitated the nomination of a third co-driver, a role Phil Mills was able to fill perfectly. In his day job he is assistant to the team's co-ordination manager, John Millington. But he is an international co-driver in his own right, and when he is not assisting with the planning of service schedules and the preparation of maps for rallies, he is navigating for the young Norwegian.

Wilson was content with his line-up. 'It was important to plan not just for 1999 but beyond, and the decision to sign three drivers to partner Colin laid a solid platform for the future, which we hope and believe will bring the reward of World Championship success,' the team director said.

chapter three

Countdown to the Championship

Even as they prepared for the 1998 Network Q (née RAC) Rally of Great Britain Colin McRae and Ford were not allowed to blot out the challenge waiting around the corner. Both parties had emotional farewells to negotiate after the concluding round of the Championship. For McRae it was a last outing with Subaru and, although he was satisfied he had made the right decision and the team acknowledged he probably had, theirs had been a long and momentous adventure. Ford, of course, were about to give their grand old lady, the Escort, a final curtsey and the occasion was accorded suitable respect.

And yet such had been the fanfare for the new alliance that it could scarcely be obliterated by the publicity machinery cranked up for this event. McRae was no longer in contention for the title. Tommi Mäkinen and Carlos Sainz would have to settle that issue. McRae v Richard Burns, signed by Subaru for 1999, provided lusty domestic material and the Scotsman was sincere enough in his declared desire for a glorious send-off. This was, after all, his home event; he had every right to deem it his domain. He had won the rally on each of his previous three attempts.

But a pre-rally Press lunch organised by Subaru reflected the train of thought. The duel with Burns dealt with, questioning inexorably turned to a life and career beyond Subaru. What did McRae make of the Focus? How about the team? Was this the change he needed? Was he eager to go testing? What was his schedule? What did he expect to achieve in 1999? Was the Championship a realistic prospect? McRae was content to answer. These matters were clearly on his mind, too. A representative of Subaru shuffled uneasily and whispered from the side of her mouth: 'We're not really here to talk about Ford.'

If he wanted to return later, he would be welcomed like a prodigal son

It was a mite awkward, although David Richards, the Subaru team principal, was gracious enough – and smart enough – to present a diplomatic hand-over. He felt it was perhaps the right time for Colin to move on and try something different, that the Scotsman had to find out for himself what he could achieve in a new environment. If, though, he wanted to return, some time in the future, he would surely be welcomed back like the prodigal son. Yes, there had been the ups and downs, but they had achieved great things together and both had benefited from the association. Subaru had become major players in world rallying and McRae was probably the best driver of the day. He had matured, learned his trade and become a more complete driver. The speed, though, was always there. And that spectacular style. Richards was proud of what he had helped make of his protégé.

McRae appeared not merely mature but positively mellow. Anyone meeting him for the first time must have wondered how this seemingly docile man could possibly be Colin McRae the rally driver, the wild man who sated his hunger for incessant thrills in his spare time by indulging in extreme sports. A phone booth sprung to mind. The PR machinery had churned out all that 'Mad Mac' stuff in his earlier days and it had paid off. It made good copy and there was, after all, a genuine streak of the daredevil in him. There has to be in every rally driver or racing driver. He wouldn't be out there otherwise.

The schedule was tight, and problems are par for this tortuous course

However, McRae, and those close to him, recognised the passage of time and other factors had brought about a change. Impending fatherhood was bound to make him more responsible. Partying into the wee hours was becoming a thing of the past. He looked forward to enjoying his limited time off as the consummate family man. He sketched the image of the quiet retreat, green meadows and livestock. He had a new perspective on life. And in any case, he didn't really have the chance to get into those crazy pursuits anymore. Maybe a spin on the bike now and then, and hopefully a bit of skiing, but that's all. It's finding the time.

Nicky Grist reckoned he'd seen the growing up process in his two years alongside McRae. 'Most of what you hear about Colin is rather out of date now,' the Welshman said. 'He has changed, as a driver and a person. He's more thoughtful about his driving. Mind you, he can still take your breath away when he wants to!'

McRae reiterated, for the umpteenth time, his conviction that Ford had offered him the opportunity he craved. Now all he wanted was to get to grips with the Focus. The Monte Carlo Rally, opening round of the 1999 World Championship, was barely a couple of months away. And he hadn't finished with his season yet. There was hardly time for a break. Yes, the team and the Focus had great potential, but he wasn't expecting too much to begin with. There were going to be inevitable teething problems. He would hope to be in a competitive situation by the middle of '99 but the Championship wasn't a realistic target, not in the first season. The aim was to get the car right, possibly pick up a couple of wins in the second half of the season, and then go for the Championship in 2000.

Over in the Ford camp, Wilson was fielding similar queries. He had to give the Escort a fitting finale while pressing ahead with the Focus programme. And although Kankkunen and Thiry were still on board, the world wanted to know about McRae. He had sheer speed, not blind courage, Wilson maintained. His great value, in an age of tight finishes, was his ability to produce the decisive last day flourish.

And about the Focus? Yes, it's coming on fine. It lends itself to rally car development. It will be aerodynamically advanced. The problem is time. (That word again.) So little opportunity to test. The Championship is not on for 1999. This is a two-year operation. The aim is 2000.

The pressure of time spawned conjecture that Wilson and his team would not be able to make the deadline to enter the Focus for 1999 and that the Escort might have to stay in service a little longer. The schedule was always going to be tight, almost unbearably so, and unforeseen problems are par for this tortuous course. One unexpected hitch was to prove particularly problematical but on 15 November 1998, the last day stipulated by the FIA, Ford presented the required homologation paperwork for the Focus World Rally Car to motorsport's governing body.

Wilson was able to direct his attention – or enough of it – to the Cheltenham event and the Escort bowed out in some style. Kankkunen was second, Thiry third, and two other Escorts finished in the top seven. There was, alas, no glorious end to McRae's career at Subaru. He was leading until his engine blew and Burns, having encountered difficulties of his own, went through to win.

'We've had to retire from the last two rallies with mechanical problems and that finished my title chances,' McRae lamented. 'This is not the way to finish the rally or my time at Subaru. I wanted to go out on a high.'

Mäkinen thought he had lost his Championship when he slid on oil dumped by a Hillman Imp in the historic competition. His Mitsubishi hit a concrete block, the impact ripping off the rear right wheel, and his attempt to reach service with one corner of the car scraping a public road was halted by a policeman on a motorbike. The Finn was packed and ready to set off for the airport on the final day when his brother called him with the news of a still more bizarre twist in the Championship tale. The engine of Sainz's Toyota expired barely 300 metres from the end of the last stage. Mäkinen had retained the title.

A bemused Mäkinen became the first driver to claim three consecutive World Championships and, although McRae rued such domination ('it would be better for the sport if the title went round more') he acclaimed Mäkinen as a true champion. Within the sport Mäkinen is considered perhaps the one driver comparable to McRae. He has pace, judgement and, naggingly for the rest, the persistence that delivers Championships.

McRae had little doubt Mäkinen and his Mitsubishi would again be at the forefront of the chase for the 1999 title. This was a proven package, a well-honed operation. They had the understanding, co-ordination and, above all, the reliability Ford would be striving to achieve in the weeks and months ahead. But then Mäkinen and his team provided the benchmark, the initial target for McRae and Ford. Their objective was to match and then surpass the standards Mitsubishi had achieved. Wilson was determined the Focus, driven by McRae, would set the standards for the future.

Anxious discussions for Wilson.

That message came through the rounds of presentations and public appearances that were somehow squeezed into the minute crevices of the 'off season'. Thomas Rådström, Simon Jean-Joseph and Petter Solberg, along with Fred Gallagher, were introduced to the media, and then McRae gave the Focus a first sample of his handling at Millbrook. He put 50 miles on the clock and expressed himself content. Wilson's relief was transparent.

'It wasn't a truly representative test because we didn't aim for that,' McRae said. 'But we weren't messing about. I was flat out. Nothing fell off and it looks ready to go out and do some proper work. I'm happy with what I've seen so far. I'm sure we can make it work.'

Wilson, who had already put the Focus through 500 miles of testing, and his team were resigned to going flat out over the Christmas and New Year period. 'There won't be many Christmas dinners eaten this year,' he said, masking the burden with a cheery countenance.

The director of Ford's rally team made scant attempt to hide his dismay the following week when he was confronted with newspaper reports suggesting the Focus would fail the FIA homologation check, scheduled for 18 December. It was alleged the governing body's working group had identified as many as 39 errors in the application, ranging from simple inaccuracies in the paperwork to suspicions about the legality of the engine. Wilson described the claims as 'pure speculation'. All, it was assumed, would be clarified when Jacques Berger, the FIA scrutineer, arrived at Millbrook to make his inspection.

Wilson recalls: 'All the parts were laid out and the night before Jacques and the FIA people were booked into a hotel. We said we'd join them later because obviously we were still flat out. Guenther and I met them for dinner and during the meal conversation turned to the water pump. Jacques asked if ours was in the standard position. We said it wasn't, we'd moved it from the front of the block, further back, off the oil pump. He said that wasn't allowed. This immediately created a huge concern. I was convinced we had an agreement on the freedom of the water pump.'

Ford had produced a larger than standard version and repositioned it in the engine bay to make the cooling more efficient. When the homologation papers were circulated to other manufacturers objections were raised. To compound Ford's plight, a breakdown of internal communications denied them the opportunity to head off the gathering storm. The team member originally assigned to consult with the governing body had left.

Time for drivers and mechanics to get down to serious work in Norway.

Ford
Valvoline

Ford
Valvoline

Wilson said: 'After the dinner I looked into the water pump situation. It had been discussed in one of the FIA technical meetings early that year. Our engineer was convinced that we had verbal agreement on freedom of the water pump. This is where the mistake lay. We did not get it confirmed in writing. Although it was noted by a number of other manufacturers, it was not in the FIA's minutes of the meeting.

'Everything else was fine. They were very complimentary about the way we'd presented all the parts. We'd passed the World Rally Car regs, it's just that we had this problem with the water pump, which was covered in the appendix, the guide to how to interpret the rules. I contacted the other manufacturers and there was a suggestion we should run at Monte Carlo but couldn't score points. Max Mosley [the President of the FIA] got involved and said that wouldn't be good for the Championship. The World Council could have changed the regulations but the other manufacturers weren't prepared to give unanimous approval, so I said we'd run under appeal.

What really upset me was the reaction of the other manufacturers

'The buck stops with me, I am responsible for the team, and it was a very difficult time for me. But I can say, categorically, there was no intention to cheat. The last thing on our mind was to do anything outside the regulations.'

Wilson was not alone in agonising over the turn of events. Martin Whitaker, the man who had taken the World Rally Championship programme out of Ford's direct care and entrusted it with M-Sport, had some explaining to do with both the media and his superiors. This incident had called into question the integrity of the company. There were, from some quarters, cries of a 'stitch up', but most observers inevitably accused Ford of a 'cock-up'. On the face of it they had been, at best, careless, at worst, reckless.

Whitaker offers some explanation: 'We, unlike any other manufacturer, had taken a two-litre, normally-aspirated engine, which developed a maximum of 160bhp, and turned it into a two-litre turbocharged engine developing just over 300bhp. Therefore, you don't need to be Einstein to work out that if you're going to change an engine that radically it's going to require different capacities and to work at different temperatures. It so happens that all the ancillary parts of the engine, such as the oil pump, alternator and a whole manner of things that are bolt-ons to the engine, are free in the regulations. The only thing that isn't free is the water pump. The law is an ass, because it's stupid that the water pump isn't free.

'So in a sense you could argue that was a mistake because amongst all the issues that were going on – and it was a highly pressurised time for us – this particular issue was forgotten by the team of designers. They were charging ahead with the design of the car and the engine, and the whole package, under the wrong impression that this interpretation of the regulations was going to be the correct one. It wasn't until 18 December, when we had the homologation, that the FIA pulled us up on the water pump.

'Under the regulations, you're supposed to use the original water pump and the original impeller, and it has to be bolted on to the engine in the same place as it is in the road car. Now, our unique mounting points, which are free, were actually at the point where the existing water pump was positioned, so it was the first thing we moved.

'After 18 December we realised we had two options. One, we could change the pump to the existing water pump, which we genuinely believed we couldn't do, because of the size and the capacity that it had to have to push water round the engine. Or two, convince the FIA that the regulations could be changed, as had happened in the past. We pursued the second option, and lost, because we weren't able to convince all the other maufacturers, which was hardly surprising.

'Seat were in a difficult position because

they had wanted to change their own water pump but had a knock-back. They wanted to rally with the Ibiza but it was marginally too short for the Championship, so they had to go with the Cordoba. In the meantime Peugeot came along, wanting to come back into the Championship. Their car was just a bit shorter than the regulations permit, but they were allowed in and Seat were quite understandably peeved.

'What really upset me was the reaction of some of the other manufacturers, and some of the things that certain manufacturers said. It was quite extraordinary. They basically accused us of cheating. Frankly that was a bit rich, particularly coming from one Japanese manufacturer who only two years previously had got slung out of the Championship for actually being caught cheating. I've always believed people who live in glass houses shouldn't throw stones, and that's what it was. I was incensed by that.'

As Ford vainly canvassed the manufacturers for unanimous support they were at least able to dispel a few other notions about their new arrival. 'The Focus doesn't have a sump problem and it doesn't have plastic windows,' Whitaker said indignantly, reacting to fanciful media speculation.

Colin McRae was preoccupied with the delivery of his own baby. Alison McRae gave birth to a girl, Hollie, on 17 December. Testing in Norway had also been a timely distraction from the maelstrom of regulations and politics. McRae drove the Focus for three days in snow and temperatures dipping to minus 20 degrees. Rådström and Jean-Joseph shared duties for the rest of the five-day stint.

'This was my first proper test with the car and I drove it really hard,' McRae said. 'I went flat out. There's no point driving any other way. It felt good and we had no major technical problems.'

The test provided the team with data for the Swedish Rally in mid-February.

A welcome break and warming camp fire.

Two further sessions were planned in the South of France ahead of the Monte Carlo Rally, which was to start on 17 January.

Progress had been made on the commercial front, too, and the Focus rally car, accompanied by McRae and Grist, was unveiled at the Autosport International Show at Birmingham's National Exhibition Centre in the distinctive and evocative livery of Martini. Few sponsors had a richer and more respected heritage in motorsport.

Martini Racing is the same age as McRae. Now the world's largest wine brand joined forces with the world's biggest rally star at Ford.

They hoped the season wouldn't explode before they had even begun competing

Bacardi-Martini director Chris Searle said: 'With the launch of the Ford Focus World Rally Car the time is right for Martini Racing to come back into world rallying. Martini have always been innovative and we think that this particular opportunity to re-enter the World Rally Championship with the Ford Focus makes it an ideal partnership for Martini Racing.'

The image was as important as the support to Ford. Whitaker says: 'One of the reasons we joined forces with Martini Racing was, of course, because all of a sudden we'd got this fantastic opportunity to raise the profile of not only our new car and Ford's new commitment but also, I believe, the profile of the sport. No disrespect to the other traditional players in the sponsorship and partnership world, but Martini has that very special aura about it. They're synonymous with success, be it with Porsche or Lancia, and really it was a great coup for us. We pushed very hard to get it.

'They bring a huge amount of promotion to the programme and the Championship. They set a different standard, I believe, in the way they go about it. It's not just directed at the specialist Press, it's directed at the lifestyle Press. Some of their advertising is very good as well. And also I think they've got, in the Focus, a rally car that gives them the opportunity to do something really eye-catching. The colour scheme we've got is very traditional, but to use the dayglo red, as we have, makes it really stand out on the stage. Martini think it's terrific.'

THIRTY YEARS OF MARTINI RACING

1968
Martini Racing make their debut race at the Hockenheim circuit. Martini & Rossi Germany are the driving force behind the first initiative.

1970
The Martini Racing Team are officially set up in London, with Wyer Engineering representing Porsche in the World Sportscar Championship.

1971
The World Sportscar Championship. The Martini & Rossi colours appear on the Porsche 917 cars. Elford and Larousse have success in the Championship, followed by Van Lennep and Marko at Le Mans.

1972
Attention turns to Formula One, choosing the Italian Tecno team from Bologna, and drivers Nanni Galli from Tuscany and Britain's Derek Bell.

1975
Martini Racing compete with two Porsche 908 cars in the World Endurance and Interseries, Peter Muller and Van Lennep at the wheel.

In Formula One Martini Racing team up with Bernie Ecclestone's victorious Brabham team. The drivers are Carlos Reutemann and Carlos Pace. Reutemann wins at the Nürburgring and is third in the championship.

1976
Brabham and Alfa Romeo team up and the cars undergo a colour change: from white to red. Hans Stuck and John

Watson succeed Reutemann and Pace, following Pace's death in an air crash.

1978
The Brabham-Martini Racing agreement ends. Martini colours continue to appear on World Prototypes and Silhouettes on the Porsche 936s and 935s. Drivers Jacky Ickx and Jochen Mass prove a winning pair. Martini take a year off from F1, and sponsor Preston and Waldegard's Porsche 911 in the Safari Rally. Preston finishes second.

The Martini Porsches continue to challenge with Ickx's 935-78 securing second place at Le Mans.

1979
Martini return to Formula One in partnership with Lotus. The cars in British racing green sport the familiar Martini colours on the upper part of the wide body. Martini split with Lotus. Involvement with endurance and rallies develops. Partnership begins with Italian company Lancia.

1981
The Beta Montecarlo driven by Alboreto and Patrese wins the Endurance title at Watkins Glen. The partnership with Lancia lasts 11 years.

1982
The Lancia Rally '037' debuts in the World Rally Championship, sporting Martini Racing colours. The mid-engined, two-wheel drive vehicle exceeds expectations in outperforming many four-wheel drive rivals.

1983
Martini Racing and Lancia triumph, securing first place in the 1983 World Rally Championship, with victories in San Remo, Monte Carlo, Corsica, Greece and New Zealand.

1987
The Lancia Deltas of Martini Racing score nine victories from 11 events.

1988
Changing to the HF Delta Integrale, the Lancia Martini Racing team again take the World Championship.

McRae geared up for the conditions.

1989
Lancia retain the world title for the third year running, and Miki Biason becomes Drivers' World Champion.

1992
Martini & Rossi's relations with the Fiat Group extend to the sponsorship of Alfa Romeo in the Italian Touring Car Championship and a return to the race track. Despite Lancia's withdrawal in 1991, Martini win the World Rally Championship with a Jolly Club-managed Delta HF.

1994
Martini Racing team up with Ford Italy and take part in the Totip Italian Championship. The Martini Racing colours dominate the '94, '95, and '96 Championships with Franco Cunico in a Ford Escort Cosworth.

1995
The colours of Martini Racing are featured on two Alfa 155 V6T1 cars in the German Touring Championship (the DTM) and the International Touring Car Championship (ITC), in 1996.

1997
Enrica Munaretto, driving a Martini Ford Escort, wins the Italian Women's Rally Championship.

1998
The Ford Martini team enter two Escort WRC cars for Franco Cunico and Angelo Medeghini. The end of year championship sees Cunico in 4th position.

1999
Martini Racing announce their partnership with Ford Racing as a challenger for the FIA World Rally Championship.

MARTINI RACING ROLL OF HONOUR
World Sportscar Champions with Porsche 1976, '77
World Sportscar Champions with Lancia 1981

The Ford Focus WRC, in Martini livery, unveiled at the NEC, Birmingham.

World Rally Champions with Lancia
1983, '87, '88, '89, '90, '91, '92
World Rally Champions (Drivers) with
Juha Kankkunen 1987, '91
World Rally Champions (Drivers) with
Miki Biason 1988, '89
Italian Rally Champions with Ford and
Franco Cunico 1994, '95, '96

The PR bit has never come as naturally to McRae as hurtling a 300bhp rally car sideways around a cliff-top bend, but he and Grist dutifully posed in front of the red, blue and white car on stage at the NEC, conducted lengthy interviews and signed endless photographs, programmes and autograph books for the captive throng.

McRae's early experience of the Focus, albeit in limited test conditions, indicated he might not have to be so sideways in this car. He found it 'closer to neutral' than his previous cars and that the low centre of gravity gave it excellent balance. The stability of the car eliminated most of the roll he might have expected. He was still, he admitted, getting used to the height of the Focus and the luxury of ample head room, even wearing a helmet.

The warm embrace of a mesmerised audience would soon give way to the harsher aspects of the job. McRae and the team knew they needed more testing, concerted testing, to give them the remotest prospect of performing competitively on the Monte Carlo. Whitaker and company, meanwhile, were tiptoeing through a political minefield in the hope their season would not blow up in their faces before they had so much as turned a wheel in anger. That scenario was a very real possibility in the countdown to the Championship.

The Ford Martini team's participation in the Monte Carlo Rally was in doubt up to the eleventh hour – literally. The controversy rumbled on into the New Year as FIA officials attempted to broker a deal that would pacify all the manufacturers in the Championship. The teams rejected the proposal of a regulation change that would have granted freedom on water pump design and location but proffered a

McRae and Grist, sitting pretty with their new baby.

Man and machine, centre of media attention.

'compromise'. They were prepared to allow the Focus to compete in the first three events with the non-standard water pump on the understanding Ford would not be able to score Championship points.

Wilson feared it might take up to two months – or three rallies into the season – to complete work on the water pump and he consistently stated he would not willingly comply with a no-points settlement. Other manufacturers publicly advised Ford to back off rather than risk the wrath of the governing body. Ford, needless to say, felt that was sanctimonious assistance they could do without. The rest of the teams did, however, agree the day before the start of the rally that if the Focus failed scrutineering they would support Ford's plea to the stewards to allow them to run their cars under appeal. The case would then go to the FIA's Court of Appeal before the next round of the Championship, the Swedish Rally, on 12 February.

At 11.30 on the morning of the Monte Carlo Rally, the Focus failed scrutineering. At midday the stewards formally excluded the cars of Colin McRae and Simon Jean-

Joseph. Ford appealed and at 12.40 the stewards agreed to let the two cars compete. At 13.52 McRae set off on the rally. At 14.00 Jean-Joseph started.

Whitaker and other Ford officials were left to field more flak from critics and rivals. Many predicted that the FIA's Court of Appeal would now come down still more heavily on Ford. They were told to expect a huge fine, possibly even suspension for their perceived insubordination, let alone the loss of any points scored on the Monte Carlo.

A stoic Whitaker said: 'Ford has been involved in rallying and other forms of motorsport for many years and has always demonstrated the highest levels of integrity and honesty in its participation. At no stage in the development of the Ford Focus rally car did we believe that the water pump system would be outside the technical regulations for the '99 WRC. Ford has at all times maintained an open approach with the FIA throughout the design and development of the Focus WRC. We look forward to a satisfactory conclusion.'

In every sense, the battle of the 1999 World Rally Championship had only just begun for the Ford Martini team.

chapter four

Flying start

It may come as a surprise to chunks of the population to discover the Monte Carlo Rally still exists. To many it is a relic of the black and white television age, its fame trapped in a time warp. A little effort will dust off vague images of Minis departing a freezing Britain, bound for the Riviera. The average non-rallying aficionado assumes the event is now staged only in reruns of clichéd old movies. The days of starting points around Europe are, indeed, long gone, but for much of the Continent this is still a focal point on their sporting landscape. Competitors and sponsors will confirm that Monte Carlo remains the most prestigious rally of them all.

To set fastest time on only the fourth stage is a big boost for the team

The principality is merely the shop window. The action is to be found on Alpine roads. As if preparation is not difficult and pressured enough for the opening round of the Championship, teams have to arm themselves for ever-changing conditions: snow, ice, even dry tarmac. The moulding of the modern World Championship event has inevitably been achieved at a price. Traditional, all-night legs have been abandoned and with them some of the sport's most evocative scenes. However, the fabled Col du Turini, where mischievous, not to say downright malicious, spectators, plied with the spirits of local hostelries, throw snow on the road to spice the show, still features prominently. The pass was to be used three times on the 1999 event.

This is often said to be Colin McRae's least favourite rally, a perception he attempts to discourage with a stoic insistence he approaches every event professionally. But as he embarked on the 1999 Monte, he cannot have been in the ideal frame of mind. Clouds of uncertainty and controversy swirled around the Focus.

Jean-Joseph was entitled to be still more apprehensive. This was only his second World Championship event. And that was not all. 'I've driven the car for only 70km in testing, it will be my first rally with a sequential gearbox, and I've never driven on a snowy rally before,' said the man from the Caribbean.

In some trepidation, Jean-Joseph followed McRae, his fellow competitor under appeal, along the road to Gap. The rally proper would begin on the Monday morning with a marathon 48km stage. The average length of the stages was more than 30km. They would be driving at rally speeds for 425km. It was a daunting baptism for the Focus and a tense experience for the team, their tangled emotions magnifying the scale of the task.

Anxiety was totally justified. That opening test almost devoured the two cars, the extreme forces of fire and ice conspiring in an unholy alliance against McRae and Jean-Joseph. The Scot lost more than two minutes with a misfire and heat from the car's exhaust melted the paint on the floor inside the car, filling the cockpit with smoke and fumes.

McRae put on a combative front: 'Without the problems we would have been fourth or fifth fastest, so that's encouraging. The black ice was incredible. I just couldn't see the icy patches.'

Neither could Jean-Joseph, dropping nine minutes on the stage. 'It was a stage I will certainly remember,' he said. 'It was slippery and we went off the road early in the stage on a slow second gear bend. We were not far off the road but the car was stuck and spectators had to help us back on. During the second half we had difficulties with the power steering, which made it difficult for me to drive at full pace.'

The pernicious conditions caught out many, including some of the more distinguished. Carlos Sainz, that paragon of consistency, crashed twice and retired. Freddy Loix went off and retired. Didier Auriol slid into a ditch and lost four minutes. Richard Burns had two offs and lost almost five minutes. The relentless Tommi Mäkinen, however, was fastest by more than a minute and the familiar benchmark was established. McRae was 14th, Jean-Joseph 40th.

Ford's drivers peeked through cracked windscreens on a more forgiving second stage, the rising ambient temperature tackling the ice. A power steering failure and broken driveshaft cost McRae more time but he was philosophical, acknowledging these were problems they were bound to encounter. A buoyant Jean-Joseph made light of a misfire and registered the eighth fastest time. He was up to 31st, McRae to 12th.

McRae's optimism about the potential of the Focus was proved justified as he completed the morning sector. He was fifth fastest, less than a second off Mäkinen's pace. Jean-Joseph was again eighth. McRae advanced to ninth overall, Jean-Joseph to 23rd. The relief restructured Malcolm Wilson's countenance. 'The great thing is that the cars are competitive,' he said. 'That means everything to me on our first event.'

McRae and Grist face up to the new challenge.

The fourth stage was likely to be less benign. The 33.82km Prunieres–Embrun test would take them to an altitude of more than 900 metres and the prospect of hostile weather. To general relief they found a mainly dry road and McRae shed any inhibitions by completing the run almost half a minute quicker than any other driver. Jean-Joseph confirmed the gathering momentum with a fourth fastest time. The rest were aghast.

'We're absolutely cock-a-hoop,' McRae said. 'To set fastest time on only the car's fourth stage is a tremendous boost for the whole team. This is a huge step forward and now we must look at doing the same on more stages.'

The final stage of that momentous Monday was the shortest of the rally, a trifling 20.35km. But the exposed nature of the St Clement–St Sauveur road advised against complacency. McRae would surely not wish to jeopardise the work and progress already accomplished. The Scotsman, sometimes said to be a law unto himself, treated the challenge with apparent disdain. He was fastest by three-quarters of a minute. He had finished the leg in sixth place, 2min 24sec behind the surprise leader, Gilles Panizzi, in a Subaru.

Turini was bad as spectators were shovelling snow onto the road

'It's been a great day,' McRae told the listening media pack, although that seemed a wholly inadequate summary. 'I'm still building my confidence with the Focus but what's good about today is that there's more to come from the car and we're already setting fastest times. Tomorrow we'll continue to learn and work on the set-up, and if we need to make modifications to improve the package we will.'

Jean-Joseph wound up his day with another top six time and 16th place overall. 'It's been a good day for me, the team and everyone involved,' he said. 'I've made some mistakes by spinning off the road a few times but I'm understanding the car and the Championship a little better. I'm happy I was on the pace of the top drivers. That is good for my personal confidence.'

Wilson beamed. 'Our main aim was to prove the Focus was competitive and those last two stages have shown that to everybody,' he said. 'The whole team has worked so hard to get us here and a look at everyone's faces tonight shows just how happy they are.'

That team includes Ford's World Rally Championship Press and PR agents, Avenue Communications, and their man back at base in Monaco, who had shared in the torment of the build-up to the rally, now shared in the elation the drivers, engineers and mechanics were experiencing up in the distant mountains. It provided a moment Mark Wilford is likely to treasure forever.

He recalls: 'When the times of those final two stages of the day came through to the media office and manufacturers' room there was initially just a silence and then this ... GASP, from all the journalists and manufacturers, because they hadn't expected us to be so quick so soon. I felt this sense of pride, sitting there, even though I'd had nothing to do with the building of the car at all. But we'd all felt involved in the overall team effort. We'd made preparations on our side as well, compiling materials for journalists, getting information out and so on. I'm not saying we were as busy as the mechanics, but we could appreciate what they felt because they'd done a lot of work over the Christmas and New Year period. And it was such a great feeling when those times came in.'

Self-congratulation soon gave way to pragmatism. A second day of competition and another heavy workload beckoned for all the team, McRae to Wilford. The drivers confronted a 14-hour leg, from Gap back to Monte Carlo. The five special stages would cover 155km. 'The crucial stage will be Sisteron–Thoard,' Nicky

McRae's drive on the Monte Carlo stuns the world of rallying.

Grist predicted. 'There's sure to be lot of snow on top of the hill so tyre choice will be vital. You must not let your choice be compromised by the snow because you need to be fast on the way up and back down again on wet asphalt.'

McRae and Grist were instantly into their stride that Tuesday morning, setting second fastest time and moving up to fourth place overall. Jean-Joseph and Fred Gallagher also advanced two positions, to 14th. The 36.72km Sisteron–Thoard stage proved less fearsome than it might have been and McRae felt confident enough to experiment on slick Michelins with small diagonal cuts. He dropped a place but consoled himself with valuable information to add to the database. Jean-Joseph eased up a further two places. McRae consolidated fifth on Stage 8, while Jean-Joseph closed in on 11th-placed Henrik Lundgaard, despite clipping a wall and damaging the car's suspension. Mäkinen regained the overall lead.

The penultimate stage of the day included the first encounter with the boisterous galleries of the Col du Turini. McRae came through the man-assisted hazard unscathed and then attacked on the final stage, recording the fastest time to go fourth on the leaderboard. Euphoria appeared to be fighting a losing battle with physical and mental fatigue.

'It's been a gruelling day,' McRae said. 'We lost time in the Sisteron stage but that was our fault because we picked the wrong tyres. Otherwise it's been good and it was great to end the day on a high with fastest time. On the previous stage Turini was bad because spectators were shovelling snow on the road. We could see where other cars had slid into the snowbanks so we were quite cautious there. That last stage was much cleaner, with better grip.'

More sympathetic spectators applauded the Ford crew after they changed a steering rack, a cross member, both front suspension uprights, a driveshaft and an anti-roll bar on Jean-Joseph's Focus in the regulation 20-minute service. He returned to Monte Carlo with 12th position and a lesson learned.

He said: 'It was a silly mistake because I had not been taking any risks. It was a long corner and I put two wheels on to the grass, which dragged the car into the

The spotlight is on McRae and the Focus for all sorts of reasons at Monte Carlo.

wall. But we've had another good day and the car has been getting better with every stage.'

McRae and Grist were subjected to a test of their mechanical acumen as well as their driving and navigating skills on the final morning. Both rear driveshafts had pulled away from the differential on the opening stage. They spun twice and lost 90 seconds but were thankful to make it to the time control. They parked by the side of the road and forced the driveshafts back into position, hoping they would hold through the next stage.

You have to wonder if there is not something perverse in the mind-set of these people. On the following stage, when prudence might have been the watchword, McRae and Grist were faster than all-comers by 20 seconds. It was their fourth quickest time of the rally and they had now elevated themselves to the top three, behind the Finns, Mäkinen and Juha Kankkunen. Jean-Joseph and Gallagher sustained their steady course to go 11th.

Competitors repeated the two stages to complete the rally and the Ford pair held their position. It had been a remarkable debut for the Focus, McRae earning his place on the podium with characteristic surges of pace, as he became accustomed to the strengths and idiosyncrasies of his new car. Jean-Joseph's performance rounded off an excellent effort by the Ford Martini team.

McRae, equalling his highest placing in the event, said: 'Never in my wildest dreams could I have imagined we'd be third in the first rally. It's a superb result for the whole team. We weren't bluffing anyone beforehand. Even after our final test in Monte Carlo I didn't feel confident about our chances. To be honest, testing had been a bit of a disaster. But the team did a lot of work while I was on the recce and came up with a revised engine and steering package that made a big difference. The really encouraging thing is that we know there is a hell of a lot more to come from the car. Everyone else had better watch out.'

Jean-Joseph won a tribute from his seasoned partner. 'He's coped extremely well with a massive learning curve during the last four days.' Gallagher said. 'Not many drivers have set a top six time on only their second ever world rally.'

Open all hours.

Wilson, who bore the brunt of the pressure through 13 months of creating and developing the Focus, said: 'It's a very emotional moment for me, more so than when the team scored their first win in Greece in 1997. After all the effort the team has put into this project, all the late nights and early mornings, to come here and get a podium place exceeds all our hopes. Colin has done an incredible job. He's a great driver and after his efforts to repair the car he's also one of our best technicians! Problems like that are to be expected with a new car but rallying is becoming so technical that it's vital to have a driver with good mechanical knowledge.'

Several months later, distanced from the emotion of the moment, Wilson gave this appraisal: 'It was the four fastest times that gave us so much satisfaction. In all honesty, we'd seen no hint of that. I'd always said I'd wanted to be competitive, even if we had technical or mechanical problems. I wouldn't have been surprised if we'd had to retire. The car had done so little real testing, one good day on asphalt. So to do that was remarkable. It was an incredible feeling.'

Whitaker, also with the benefit of perspective, echoed that incredulity: 'When the car caught fire in the first stage I thought, "Oh my goodness, this is it." We always imagined the first half of the year was going to be very, very difficult. It was a brand new car and we went to Monte Carlo having done very limited testing. And when I say testing I mean, for the most part, driving it up and down in a straight line at Millbrook. So we hadn't really driven the car. But once we'd overcome the first couple of stages Colin started setting fastest times and it was just the most amazing performance.'

Except, of course, the team still had to fight their appeal against exclusion from the rally, and the issue of the water pump tempered some of the acclaim for Ford's achievement. Certain critics dismissed the car as illegal, the result as meaningless. More balanced observations accepted there probably had been little or no performance advantage gained from the water pump but that nevertheless the FIA had to apply the letter of the law and strip Ford of their points.

Rådström appreciates the dubious home comforts of the Swedish Rally.

McRae, having produced that third place against seemingly impossible odds, was in no mood to accept the inevitability of such a decision that evening in Monte Carlo and was already venting his frustration over the affair.

'I'll be the victim if they take the points away from me, but I don't think it will come to that,' he said, endeavouring to bolster his optimism. 'At the end of the day it is Ford's mistake, but it doesn't give the car a performance advantage. It's just a water pump.'

That first sign of dissension would be seized upon by a diligent journalist when the FIA Court of Appeal rejected Ford's case and upheld the decision of the Monte Carlo stewards. The team, and McRae, duly lost their points but no other punishment was meted out to Ford, who undertook to modify their cars in line with the regulations and compete at the Swedish Rally, starting only 11 days later.

Jeremy Hart, who writes for *The Times*, *The Mirror* and *Sunday Mirror*, reported McRae's angry reaction. 'I'm not happy about this,' the Scotsman told Hart. 'It's disappointing to lose the points after what was a great drive. It's a kick in the guts after all the effort I've put in since the end of the RAC Rally to have it taken away. The team needs to sort this out and we need to come back. I don't know if it will be in Sweden. I don't know when it will be. I'm gutted.

'I'm disappointed in Ford and M-Sport. It's not acceptable. It's just a homologation issue, but it's a major mistake on behalf of a lot of engineers. It was still the right decision to go to Ford, but you don't know about these kind of things at the time.'

It was not what Ford and M-Sport needed to read as they attempted to pick themselves off their knees. But this was authentic McRae. Over the course of a fortnight they had seen him at his best and also at his most vulnerable, when the rebel in him rises to the bait. He, in turn, discovered the sterner side of his taskmaster.

Whitaker said: 'That did cause ripples, not least from my senior management, because they saw things from a different perspective and quite rightly so. We rapped Colin over the knuckles for that.

Wilson and Gallagher plot Solberg's steady course.

Solberg follows his instructions to the letter.

He said something to the effect that Ford's engineers hadn't got a clue what they were doing. What they actually were doing was pretty clever. They were interpreting the regulations to our best advantage, and that's what you do as an engineer and a designer. Colin had perhaps been protected from that side of the business and that was probably our fault. We perhaps hadn't immersed him enough in what was going on at that level. You live and learn and I think he learned a lot from that.

'It also came at a time of the year when the sport was quiet, and we got an incredible amount of interest and coverage. It was another demonstration of the feeling and emotion involved. In a sense the whole thing became even worse after Monte Carlo because everybody started saying we had only done as well as we had because we had an illegal water pump, which was absolute balderdash. It wasn't the water pump that was making us go quicker, but that's what they thought and that's why subsequent success was sweeter still.

'We employed a barrister and did everything we could to present our case to the FIA Court of Appeal, and although we lost our points for Monte Carlo we weren't fined, which I think was the important thing. We were open with everybody, we were never dishonest with anybody about what we were doing. We never tried to do anything which was illegal, we didn't try to cheat or anything of that nature, and that was recognised by the FIA Court of Appeal.'

Comforting though that was, Wilson and his team still had the onerous – if not, as they feared, impossible – task of reconstructing the engine bay of the Focus with a standard water pump, and all under a lingering shadow of suspicion.

'There was a big cloud hanging over me and all the staff,' Wilson confides. 'It was a horrible situation to be in. We hadn't got the unanimous support we would have liked from the manufacturers but I told the team we couldn't go to Sweden and Safari with this still hanging over us. There's no question it made us even more determined to show them. OK, we lost the appeal, but I feel that was the closest we were ever going to get to a victory so I was relieved about that. And the FIA did a good job in hearing the case as soon as possible after Monte Carlo.

'The workload it gave us was unbelievable. Up until the night before the cars left for Sweden we had major, major problems redesigning, rebuilding, everything. I didn't think it would be possible to make it. We were very close to not turning up in Sweden. No-one outside the team was aware how close. It was getting to the point where we talked about going over the ramp and then stopping, just to avoid a fine for not competing. Fortunately we managed to get a bit further than that.

'It was a massive, non-stop job. The Cologne end of Ford got involved and they were really helpful in calculating the best possible way to get the flow right for the standard pump, how to reposition the outlet to make it more efficient. And when the work was finished we were able to kill off all those claims about horsepower because we actually gained 0.6 of a kilowatt by running a standard water pump. It proved there had been no performance advantage at all.'

Whitaker's anxiety before Sweden was equally acute. 'We genuinely didn't know whether the car would get to Sweden, but we realised if we didn't start it would have been a disaster for us. Our season could have been over before it had even started. So we discussed the possibility of just crawling over the start ramp, getting round the corner and then pulling out. You can imagine trying to convey that message to senior management. I lived, breathed, slept and ate water pumps for the best part of six weeks. We were all under a lot of pressure. But I always felt we would eventually get it right. By then I had a lot of faith not only in Malcolm but more importantly in his design team. And the engine guys from Mountune also did a fantastic job.'

Ford kept most of their pre-Sweden problems to themselves and McRae confined his comments to positive prospects for the Championship's only genuine winter rally. Temperatures can plunge to as low as –25°C on this event. Studded tyres are essential and the use of roadside snowbanks is a skill long perfected by Nordic drivers.

McRae was less comfortable and had to accept a secondary role

'The stages are fast but very forgiving if you make a mistake,' McRae said. 'You can use the snowbanks to position and balance the car in the corners. It's important to adjust your driving style to compensate for the snow and ice, remembering to do everything much earlier than you would on gravel and asphalt. Nordic drivers have dominated this rally but there's no reason why. I've been close to winning a couple of times and it's far less specialised than Finland.'

Thomas Rådström, taking over from Jean-Joseph and making his scheduled debut in the Focus, had every right to be optimistic, given a properly functioning car. He won his home event in 1994, when it did not have World Championship status, won the national title in 1996 and led the 1998 Swedish Rally for a day and a half before having to retire.

He said: 'People tell me how amazed they are that Scandinavian drivers have such car control in snowy conditions. But we're born in these conditions, we live in these conditions and we drive in them for five months of the year. There's no big secret to driving quickly on snow and ice – just stay in the ruts and use the snowbanks.'

Ford had a second debutant in Petter Solberg, the 24-year-old Norwegian partnering Phil Mills in an M-Sport prepared Ford Escort.

It was ironic that after all the controversy and heartache caused by Ford's quest for a more efficient cooling system that they should now be faced with the problem of keeping their engines warm enough to operate to their full potential. The trick is to close the thermostat connected to the radiator for much of the time, so reducing the flow of cold water into the engine. The build-up of ice on the cars is another particular problem to Sweden. Mechanics remove as much of it as possible at services to ensure engine power and traction are not wasted. The rally, based in Karlstad, covers 384 stage kilometres.

To the relief of everyone in the Ford camp, both McRae and Rådström negotiated not merely the start ramp and first corner, but the entire opening stage. McRae was a satisfactory fifth fastest, Rådström a splendid second behind Sainz. Solberg was tenth. Mäkinen leapfrogged Rådström and Sainz on the second stage but McRae held fifth position. Solberg was 11th.

Rådström was fortunate to avoid serious damage when he hit a frozen tree stump on Stage 3 but went on to set the fastest time through the 21.58km of Bjalverud and completed the opening leg in third place. 'The conditions on the stages are really good and if they stay like that for tomorrow I'll be able to attack hard,' he said. 'But I'm also a bit angry with myself because I twice stalled on the startline of stages. If you look at the time we lost from that we would have been even closer to the front.'

McRae was less comfortable and had to accept a secondary role. He lost almost a minute on the sixth stage but finished the day retaining a respectable fifth. 'We came over a crest and dropped the left rear wheel into a ditch,' he said. 'We must have hit a rock because it smashed the wheel and we had to drive the final seven kilometres with the car running on the brake disc.'

Solberg admitted to a wrong tyre choice but he, too, was still there after the first day, in 11th place.

McRae, alas, was no longer in the rally after the first stage of the second day. An engine problem brought the Focus to a halt midway through the 14km Sagen test. 'We had just decided to pull over to have a look under the bonnet when the engine lost all compression and stopped,' McRae said.

Rådström, appreciating the concentrated effort on his car, consolidated his third place and planned to intensify his attack on the final day. 'We have to be in a position to make the most of any mistakes by the two drivers ahead of us,' the Swede said.

By the final stage, however, Rådström was more concerned with the man looming large in his mirrors, Didier Auriol. The Frenchman had closed to within 4.3 seconds before the 22km home run. The Ford team provided Rådström with a lighter car by removing the jack, spare wheel, tool kit and drinks bottles, and that initiative just might have made the difference. Rådström made it on to the podium, behind Mäkinen and Sainz, by 2.5 seconds. And this time the points were secure.

Rådström said: 'I was quite nervous before the final stage but I decided I had to drive harder than I had on any other stage because I knew Didier would. The car was right on the limit throughout the stage. The car has been a pleasure to drive and I feel fantastic. Fred and I have settled in well together on our first event and I can't wait for the next rally.'

Gallagher was evidently impressed. 'He's extremely talented,' the co-driver said. 'He reminds me of Bjorn Waldegard. If he's half as successful I'll be happy.'

Wilson could scarcely have been more content. He had come through the darkest of winters into this white wonderland. 'Thomas has driven superbly and I knew from the look on his face when he left the service park for the final stage there was just no way he was going to allow Didier to beat him,' the team boss said. 'After Monte Carlo it was important that we showed similar speed and reliability here. To finish on the podium is fitting reward for everybody in the team.'

Solberg produced the solid performance required of him to finish 11th. McRae may have been the odd man out

McRae and Ford leave behind the clouds of suspicion with victory on the Safari.

this time but he looked ahead to Safari with faith and optimism restored. 'There's no reason to be despondent,' he said. 'In fact, we may have to revise our predictions about when we'll win our first event. It could be mid-year rather than later.'

The Swedish effort had galvanised a team that might have crumbled. 'Everybody needed a lift after all that had happened and that rally provided it,' Wilson says. 'It was a great result for Thomas and the team. The car ran without anything dropping off. Colin's car overheated and that was down to one of the few parts we used from the Escort. It did the head gasket.'

You can only surmise as to the effect on Wilson's head when his meticulous planning was derailed again two days after the Swedish Rally. Rådström, who along with McRae had flown from Sweden to Kenya to prepare for the Safari, fell in the reception area of the team's hotel, breaking his lower left leg in two places. This was becoming a jinx rally. Bruno Thiry had to be replaced 12 months earlier. Now Wilson can throw up his eyes and smile about the mini crisis.

It was like driving in hell – the stones were so big in there

'They were doing up the hotel, there were ramps instead of steps, and anyway Thomas slipped and made a real mess of his leg,' Wilson says. 'And it's the day before the recce! The year before Bruno smashed his ribs and I had to draft in Ari [Vatanen]. As you can imagine, the news travelled like wildfire. My telephone was red hot and Ari was the first to call me.

'But this time I thought, "No, I'm going to put the young boy, Petter, in." Phil Mills had been Petter's co-driver in Sweden but I felt that for the Safari there would be no better person for him to sit with than Fred. I gave Fred complete control, even to the point where he asked if he was allowed to hit the boy if he was going too fast. I told him to do whatever he felt fit. Petter just had to drive round and finish the rally.'

Solberg had to be scrambled from Norway – where he was due to compete in a local event, the Finnskog Rally – and catch a plane to Nairobi. McRae, meanwhile, had his teeth into the job and Wilson sensed he was not about to let go. Neither man was perturbed that McRae had broken his right thumb on the steering wheel when he hit a tree stump in the recce and had to have it strapped.

Wilson says: 'I went out and watched the last couple of days of the test and saw Colin driving flat out and I thought, "Yes, this is looking good." I actually said at the Press conference I felt we could possibly win. Inside me I knew we had a real chance.'

The Safari remains the great adventure of the Championship, the ultimate test of reliability and durability in the eyes of the manufacturers. Win here and you prove a point. Pot-holed, dusty roads and intense heat present very different problems from those posed in Sweden. No rally is more physically demanding for a driver. Cars are reinforced to withstand the ordeal and fitted with 'roo bars' for additional protection in the event of a collision with wildlife. A 'snorkel', leading from the engine to roof level, allows air to reach the unit when the car is in flood water. Spotter helicopters warn villagers of approaching rally cars and drivers of roaming animals.

Such hazards were unlikely on the rally's overture, a short super special stage. Much ado about nothing. McRae was fourth, Solberg tenth. The rally proper began the following morning, drivers bracing themselves for fast open stretches and rocky first gear snares. McRae was unamazed and unabashed by a puncture. He damaged the front sub-frame when he hit a rock on the third stage and admitted: 'I can't believe we're still going after that impact.' The lead Focus had two more punctures on the next stage but this time its tyres contained mousse and Grist was spared the task of changing them. They finished the day in third place, with Solberg and Gallagher seventh.

Solberg was learning about the Safari the hard way. 'We had to drive for more than 20km in another car's dust,' he said. 'It was so bad at one point that we went off the road and into a ditch. We just couldn't see where we were going. Fred's experience had been invaluable.'

The threat of Fred's backhander presumably helped concentrate the mind. The following morning Solberg had to focus his attention as never before, encountering what he described as 'the worst stage of my life.' He took no risks and emerged eighth overall.

McRae, equipped with a stiffer suspension setting, moved up to second after Sainz had three punctures and dropped more than eight minutes. Ahead of the Scot was the Englishman Richard Burns in a Subaru. McRae was frustrated to lose time in the Spaniard's dust, but the rally tilted his way on the next stage. A bolt broke on the front suspension of Burns's car and he had to pull out. A spin could not deprive McRae of first place. 'The road was so narrow there that it needed a lot of manoeuvring to point the car in the right direction,' he said.

Solberg was finding his bearings with fifth fastest time on the stage. A puncture on the day's penultimate stage put him back and he was seventh again overnight. McRae was in the lead by an astonishing 14min 46.4sec over Mäkinen. Judicious driving and the reliability of the Focus had given him a clear view of his maiden victory with Ford, and yet he declined to tempt providence.

'It's too early to start talking about winning,' he protested. 'We've got a good lead but we've seen on many occasions on this rally how easy it is to lose 10 or 15 minutes in a section. We're feeling confident about tomorrow but this rally is so unpredictable that I'm sure there are more shocks and surprises in store.'

McRae headed for the foothills of Mount Kilimanjaro on the final morning of the Safari intent on using that huge advantage. He restrained his natural instincts and the team turned down the turbo boost pressure of the Focus. Even after a puncture and deferring to a herd of cattle, they still came through the day's first two stages with a 10-minute lead.

Victory on only their third rally for McRae, Grist and the Focus.

Piero Liatti's retirement promoted Solberg to a point-scoring sixth place.

Both drivers snaked their way around the boulders of the last authentic stage. 'It was like driving in hell,' Solberg said. 'The stones were so big in there.'

Only a repeat run of the 2.42km super special stage lay between the Ford pairings and a result the team would greet as vindication and therefore all the more precious. McRae duly completed his part of the mission, beating Mäkinen by 7min 49.1sec. Solberg was an equally comfortable sixth. He was subsequently given fifth place after Mäkinen's disqualification for 'receiving outside assistance' when spectators helped him change a wheel.

This is a new car and a new team and that makes this very special

McRae had his second Safari win, Ford the first on the event since 1977. More significantly, in the eyes of the rallying world, the Focus was a winner on only its third outing.

'This means more to me than my first Safari win,' McRae said. 'This is a new car and a new team, and that makes this very special. This last day has been one of the most nerve-racking I've ever had because on the Safari you can never guarantee anything until it's over. This is a good indicator for the rest of the season. The engineers have done a fantastic job in designing the car. Over the last few months we've experienced big highs and big lows, but this is the biggest high of all.'

Solberg was in a daze. 'I'm finding it really hard to take this in,' he said. 'We came out here firstly with the aim of trying to finish the rally and secondly of going for a top 10 place. To score points is a great feeling.'

Wilson talked of the emotion of the moment but the satisfaction is interminable.

'I'd always wanted to win the Safari, and to have two cars in the points, especially in the circumstances, was brilliant, just brilliant,' Wilson says. 'But the real thrill for me was knowing how much it meant to other manufacturers. To them the Safari is still THE rally to crack, it is more important to them than any other in the Championship. It's the tradition, it's not modern day rallying. It's something they've known for years, and we won it. It was an incredible result.'

It was also powerful evidence for Whitaker to put before his senior management at Ford. 'After all the flak we'd had from other manufacturers it was such sweet success,' he says. 'OK, we know the Safari can be a bit of a lottery, but you must not take anything away from that win. As we're always told in motorsport, to finish first, first you have to finish. And in a sense Petter's result was even better than Colin's. He'd never been there before, he was rushed to the rally at the last minute, and he did an immaculate job.'

McRae, as we often hear, always did like a party and he discovered kindred spirits in the Ford camp that evening in Nairobi. This was a team triumph and the celebrations provide another gem for Wilford's souvenirs.

'At the end of the rally we went to the prize presentation at the HQ hotel,' he says. 'We had a meal outside and of course it wasn't long before people were being thrown in the pool. We all trooped out of the hotel, dripping wet, looking for a taxi back to our hotel. The taxi driver took one look at us and shook his head. I said to him, "But this is Colin McRae, he's just won the Safari Rally." Suddenly a big beam came across his face. He threw open the doors, opened the boot and we had 13 people in the taxi, including Colin, all dripping wet, plus all the trophies. He took us across Nairobi and we all tumbled out at the other end. I asked him how much I owed him and he said, "No, no, my pleasure, my pleasure." He drove off with a drenched taxi, still beaming.'

chapter five

Title trail

Derision had turned to admiration. Grudging admiration in some quarters but admiration nonetheless. The consensus was that Ford had produced a car capable of winning more rallies in 1999 and, in the hands of Colin McRae, had to be a serious contender for the Championship. This rapid transformation of circumstances unnerved Malcolm Wilson. He went to Portugal fearing a rude awakening from this fantasy.

'For the next one I have to say I was really apprehensive,' Wilson confesses. 'We'd had a fantastic run in Safari and I thought to myself, "This is going to be the reality shock." I had very little confidence at all. Our cars were 70 to 80 kilos heavier than the opposition's and the stages were in good condition. So it was going to be a sprint rally and we were going to struggle.'

A buoyant McRae made no concession to his boss's sensitivities. Asked if he now believed he was in the frame for the title, he felt he had to respond in the affirmative.

'I think the Championship is a realistic goal,' he said. 'I certainly haven't ruled out winning it. The Championship was always in the back of my mind but we thought it would take us the first half of the year to make the Focus truly competitive. Another top three finish is definitely a possibility but the question is whether we have the edge yet to fight for victory on a sprint-type gravel rally. The car is heavier than we would like.'

Petter Solberg, again deputising for the indisposed Rådström, was anticipating a more comfortable ride on this, the season's first true all-gravel event and an acknowledged indicator of how the Championship is likely to pan out. The unleashed enthusiasm of the spectators can be as perilous on this rally as the rocks, floods and wildlife of Safari.

Martin Whitaker, privy to Wilson's concerns, was content to stand up another, more positive story for the intrepid Hart, who reported that McRae was to test the Stewart Ford Formula One car and might switch to Grand Prix racing.

I said when we won Kenya I was lost for words and I am again today

Whitaker recalls: 'I was there for the first day of the rally and I thought that since we were not going to do very well I might as well get us a bit of exposure by going along with the Formula One line. Having said that, I have always believed the great rally drivers are just as, if not more, talented than Grand Prix drivers. I've always said the greatest Spanish Grand Prix driver has never driven a Grand Prix, and that's obviously Carlos Sainz. They are probably more complete racing drivers. So this was an opportunity to endorse what I'd said before, and it was absolutely true.

'We'd always said we'd wanted to give Colin a run in a Formula One car, perhaps in a way to back up what we'd always thought about him. But also it's a promotional tool, no doubt about that. You do things like that for the promotional value. Jeremy asked if it would be done for a bit of fun but I said it wouldn't, that everything we did was done seriously. You can't shove anyone in a Grand Prix car any more. Nowadays these things are pretty serious technological pieces of kit, so you have to undertake every test in a very serious way. The story got rather blown up out of all proportion. Colin won't be switching permanently. But having taken that opportunity to hit the headlines we did so again in the rally.'

Solberg rises to the occasion in Portugal, encouraged by typically enthusiastic spectators.

McRae revelled in the theatre of the short, head-to-head super special stage to take an instant lead, albeit by a meagre four tenths of a second. Even the dust, which found its way through the roof ventilation holes, could not wipe the smiles off the faces of McRae and Grist. The fun, they conceded, would have to give way to earnest rallying the following morning.

Solberg, reunited with his regular partner, Phil Mills, wasn't laughing anyway. He stalled on that show stage and was 18th fastest, 10.1 seconds behind his teammate.

Frivolous or serious, it all seemed the same to McRae now. He was fastest on five of the first full day's stages, opening a lead of 49.2 seconds over Richard Burns. He attacked from the start and appeared to catch the rest cold. It was not an entirely trouble-free day. Mechanics had to replace a cracked windscreen and the tyre mousse kept him going after he hit a rock, the force of impact gouging a chunk out of the rubber and wheel rim.

'It's been a superb day,' McRae was able to say without fear of contradiction. 'After the tests we knew the car would be quick on this type of surface, but I'm surprised just how quick it's been today. I don't think running first through tomorrow's stages will be a problem because the roads are not too dusty and loose.'

And this in a car Wilson thought would be far too heavy to achieve its optimum performance and muster a genuine challenge to the regular front-runners of the Championship. Wilson was struggling to make sense of it all.

'I said when we won in Kenya that I was lost for words and I am again today. There's no way I expected the car to be this quick. Our times in testing were good compared with last year's but everyone makes progress. Colin pushed very hard on the first two stages this morning and then controlled things from the front. I would like him to adopt the same tactics in the morning.'

Solberg, acclimatising to the pace and technical intricacies of a sprint-type rally, was a more subdued 14th.

'Some drivers here have competed on this rally seven or eight times,' he reasoned. 'This is only my fifth World Championship event and my first on smooth gravel like this, so it's a big learning experience. We dropped around 20 seconds on the last stage after a spin and had a few problems when the car started jumping out of gear, but once that was fixed it was like driving a new car again.'

McRae demonstrated he could be disciplined, adhering to Wilson's strategy and doing just enough to retain a comfortable advantage. He lost rather more time than he would have liked on stage 17, which he blamed on wheelspin and subsequent tyre wear. His lead over second placed Sainz was 33 seconds. 'We'll try to pull a few seconds back on the final two stages and give us a good cushion for tomorrow,' he said.

He was denied the opportunity. Crowds on those two tests had swollen to unmanageable proportions and both were cancelled for safety reasons, trimming more than 40km off the scheduled 180km leg.

'It's been a very mature, very sensible drive by Colin,' Wilson enthused. 'The time loss suffered by being first on the road has not been as significant today as in previous years. Last night we calculated how much time our rivals might take back today and the actual figure is far less than we anticipated. I said we needed to have a lead of 30 seconds tonight and Colin is 33 seconds in front so we're happy.'

Solberg was a little more sanguine that evening, having made a steady ascent to 10th and established a firmer foothold.

'We're learning more about this rally with every stage, but we still have a lot

McRae emerges triumphant from his test of nerve and discipline in Portugal.

more to discover,' he said. 'The car has been perfect today and my confidence has been improving steadily. Tomorrow I must concentrate on holding my position.'

McRae might have echoed the sentiment. He allowed Sainz, under pressure from Auriol, to gnaw at his advantage but still had 20.5 seconds in hand as they lined up for the last of the day's four stages. The Scotsman merely had to avoid error and hazard for another 15.85km to claim a second successive victory.

He said: 'The first two stages this morning were on a good, hard surface but the last one was very soft and sandy, and getting good traction was difficult. We lost a little time but nothing to worry about. We're still driving hard but not at 100 per cent and I'm confident about the final stage.'

McRae and Grist are getting the hang of this.

With justification. McRae finished this tour of northern and central Portugal as he had begun it, with utter conviction. His winning margin over Sainz was 12.3 seconds. It was his 18th World Championship victory, leaving him just four behind the Spaniard's record total. The others can only have wondered how much McRae had in reserve, and how much more was to come from the Focus given further development and a reduction in weight. As it was, he advanced to second place in the Drivers' Championship, just two points behind Mäkinen. Ford were second in the manufacturers' standings, five points behind Toyota.

'Championship' could no longer be a taboo word. Wilson's misgivings had been proved unfounded, as he was willing to concede. 'To win in Kenya was marvellous but to win here, on a gravel event where outright speed counts for everything, is very special. The Focus ran like clockwork and that's encouraging for us. We'll now look at restructuring our strategy for the next four rallies. We'll run only two cars and put everything into helping Colin's chances of winning the drivers' series.'

McRae and Grist were less impressed with the clockwork of the officials and Grist had a spat with a marshal on the second stage of the second full day. 'The start clocks were out by 25 seconds,' the Welshman explained. 'I wasn't having any of that. The marshal changed the time on my card but we still lost probably four or five seconds.'

Nothing, however, could divert McRae from his assured course. 'We really won the rally on the first leg, when we knew we had to make the most of the good conditions,' he said. 'It's been much harder than many of my other victories but the Focus has performed faultlessly. For the car to be this quick on gravel means it can also be this good on asphalt, so I think the rest of the season could be well worth waiting for.'

Solberg's topsy-turvy rally took a final tumble when he flipped the car on its side and was relegated to 11th overall. 'I'm annoyed I missed out on a top 10 position,' he said. 'The damage was not great but it cost me that place by less than four seconds. This has been a hard rally for me and again it was important to finish, and learn as much as possible. The first two legs were difficult and my spirits were a little low, but my times improved and my confidence increased.'

Whitaker's other commitments had compelled him to return to his office after the first day of the rally and sweat through the ordeal behind his desk.

'I was sitting listening to the results coming through after every stage and it was getting closer and closer. But Colin made it and at the end, I make no bones about it, I completely dissolved. Safari was great but I think Portugal was even better. For me it was incredibly moving. And it was certainly tearful. I was completely choked up in the office. I think a lot of other people were as well. To win back-to-back, and to lead from the very start, the way Colin had done, was tremendous. It was probably his greatest rally. It perhaps convinced people he was worth the money. I always was.'

On reflection, midway through 1999, Wilson, too, contends it was the finest rally of McRae's life.

'He was simply magnificent. The first two stages of the rally are very technical and he put a lot of work into them and realised if he really went for it he could make a lot of time. He did that and controlled the rally from there on. That, to me, makes it his most professional rally to date. He ran at the front, the first car on the road for the second and third days, coped with the pressures, the new car, all the hype surrounding it, and never put a foot wrong.'

Wilson and his team now had to address the problem of the car's weight. 'It's probably costing us 0.3 to 0.4 seconds a kilometre, he said, and estimated the development and materials necessary to shed that 70kg excess would cost £2m. The immediate objective was to trim perhaps 30kg before the Catalunya Rally, an asphalt event which favours the nimble. That additional weight is not such a handicap when the car can be flicked sideways through gravel corners, but on tarmac it is always apparent under braking and on tyre wear. McRae was on the title trail and Wilson recognised the team had to feed his motivation. Come the Spanish event, he was able to report a weight loss of almost 40kg.

Wilson said: 'So far this season we've concentrated on making the car reliable and that's paid dividends. Since Portugal we've put extra emphasis on performance and our engineers have been working

Jean-Joseph prepares for action in Spain.

hard to reduce the weight by using lightweight materials where we can. We'll use forged magnesium wheel trims, we've rerouted the pipework using lighter hoses, we've lost weight from the roll cage without compromising safety and adopted lighter underbody protection, which is just as strong. The weight loss will obviously affect the car's set-up but we have enough allowance in the suspension to alter the damper settings to compensate.'

Catalunya represented a final journey into the unknown for the Focus. It had made imperious progress across snow, ice, rocks and gravel. If it now conquered this all-asphalt domain then nothing would be beyond its powers.

McRae said: 'This will be the last telltale rally for the Focus. When we tested in Spain our times compared favourably with testing on the same roads last year. Although the car is still heavier than our rivals' I'm confident we can finish in a podium position again.'

McRae on a testing mission at the Catalunya Rally.

Simon Jean-Joseph, the team's asphalt specialist, returned to active duty pleasantly surprised by the improvement in the Focus.

He said: 'Since Monte Carlo the engine, gearbox and driveability have all improved and the car feels very stable, which is exactly what you need for an asphalt event. Conditions in Spain should suit me better than Monte Carlo, but as I've not driven this rally before one of the biggest difficulties will be to develop a good set of pace notes because we have so little opportunity to practise.'

McRae, Jean-Joseph and every other driver except Tommi Mäkinen was spared the first scheduled stage for safety reasons. The characteristic exuberance of the Spanish fans got the better of them and many spilled over the barriers on to the edge of the road. McRae was particularly relieved. The second stage exposed a misjudgement on tyre choice by the Scotsman. He was seventh fastest, Jean-Joseph 11th.

That first actual test confirmed Ford's

concerns about weight. Fastest was Spain's Jesus Puras, driving a Formula Two Citroën Xsara. It was one of four lightweight two-wheel drive cars in the top ten. Leading teams argued it was an unacceptable state of affairs. In truth it was embarrassing for the Championship. At least the World Rally Cars were competing against each other on a level playing field and Ford had to carry the fight to familiar rivals.

Halfway through that opening day McRae was up to sixth, but an engine fault cost him nearly six minutes over two stages. He tumbled to 39th and, he had to concede, out of contention for a third consecutive win. He was 33rd at the end of the leg and even a points-scoring position was an unlikely prospect. So McRae and the team decided to cut their losses and utilise the rest of the event as a test ahead of another asphalt rally, the Tour of Corsica.

The engine problem was traced to a valve failure in the anti-lag system, which prevented the turbocharger from developing full boost pressure. McRae was left with the power he would expect from the Ford Focus road car rather than a £350,000 300bhp World Rally Car.

'Until that happened I felt we were in contention for a top three finish,' he said. 'If we now use the rally to test it will be a big benefit for Corsica. We haven't done a lot of asphalt testing so this is a good opportunity to do just that.'

Jean-Joseph gradually had the car's handling to his liking, reached the overnight halt in 12th place and declared his intention to raise his game the following day.

McRae had no other thought on his mind. He was fastest on two stages, second fastest on another. His second day performance was eclipsed only by Philippe Bugalski in another lightweight two-wheel drive Citroën. McRae officially withdrew at the end of the day, by which time Jean-Joseph had retired with an alternator problem after climbing into the top ten.

Wilson was consoled by McRae's times: 'His test work has been absolutely invalu-

More impressive work behind the wheel.

able. We've gained a lot of knowledge from this afternoon's 46km stage. We're happy we have a good base set-up for Corsica but the test has shown up other aspects we need to address and we're keen to get back to England to look at these. This is the busiest time of the season and with three rallies in the next five weeks we want to use the time to work on the car.'

Wilson now reveals how he persuaded McRae to undertake that unscripted test. 'I had to go to him at the end of the first day and say, "Look, Colin, we need to continue tomorrow, to test. If we're going to win the Championship you're going to have to continue." Once he saw what we were trying to achieve he was great. And of course he went out the next day, did a fantastic job, and gave us more information and ideas for Corsica. That's the most I've ever got out of Catalunya! I still haven't scored a point there in three attempts with a factory team. It's my bogey rally.'

Bugalski's win softened the blow to McRae's Championship aspirations. Mäkinen's third place gave him a total of 26 points and Auriol, second on the event, moved on to 23 points, three ahead of the Ford driver.

The Ford Martini team headed for the Mediterranean island of Corsica convinced they were better prepared for this tarmac examination. That impromptu test session in Catalunya had given them a fresh insight into the requirements and the drivers had good vibes about the event. McRae had won it twice and this was the only World Championship rally Jean-Joseph had competed in before he joined Wilson's team.

Typically, however, there were still a few late jobs to be completed and any member of the team may be called upon to lend a hand. Gavin Green, newly appointed UK-based head of communications for Ford Racing, found himself with excess baggage for the flight to Corsica.

'I got a call from M-Sport wondering if I could bring out four anti-roll bars because they were too late to go in the truck,' he says. 'I was the last team member to go out and their only way of getting them there. They said the anti-roll bars would be helicoptered down from Cumbria to Millbrook, and taken from there to Heathrow by Philip Baker [the sponsor co-ordinator] who would meet me there. They said they would be light and I'd be able to carry them on as hand luggage. It sounded very unlikely but I was obviously not going to say no.

'So I met Philip at Heathrow and the first thing he said was, "They are a bit bigger than I thought." He took me round the corner to a trolley, on which were four extremely large anti-roll bars, two sets of two. And they weighed A LOT. As soon as I showed them to the girl at the check-in she said I certainly couldn't take them on as hand luggage because they were so big and of such an unusual dimension. They would have to go in oversize baggage. So we went to the oversize baggage point and the girl there wanted to know what on earth I'd got. And of course she'd no idea what anti-roll bars were. Anyway, I eventually checked them in for the hold of the aircraft, marked to Corsica, via Nice, where I was changing planes, and they duly made it. I'm not sure, though, whether they were actually used.'

Much pre-rally discussion centred on the introduction of a final stage packaged specially for television. The 13.82km test would carry additional points – three, two and one – for the three fastest drivers. More contentious still, official team drivers who had retired from the event would be allowed to contest this last stage. Twenty cameras on the ground, ten in cars and two on helicopters would give a glimpse of rallying in the future – at a cost of around £260,000.

The scenery on the rugged French island is stunning but admiring glances from drivers can have catastrophic consequences. The event is respectfully known as 'The Rally of 10,000 Corners'. Tyre

McRae resists the distractions of the views on the Tour of Corsica.

Ford
MARTINI
Valvoline

McRae (left) makes a splash in Argentina …

… while Rådström (above) is thrown in at the deep end …

… and it's Thomas who comes up smiling.

care is critical. The tight, twisty roads have a notoriously abrasive surface.

McRae made a confident start, setting fastest time on the opening stage. He dropped to fifth after the second, behind François Delecour in the new Peugeot 206, Bugalski and Puras in THOSE Citroëns, and Sainz in the Toyota. Ford's senior driver was still fifth at the end of the day, by which time Bugalski had the overall lead.

Jean-Joseph's rally lasted less than five kilometres. 'The car cut out completely and we were unable to restart,' he said.

The competition was tight, ripe for someone to exploit with a sudden surge

Wilson expressed satisfaction with McRae's position: 'We're the only four-wheel drive manufacturer to have set a fastest time. Colin's in a strong overall position and we will be in a good place on the road for tomorrow's leg. We made a wrong tyre choice for the first couple of stages. Ironically Colin set fastest time on the first but the soft compound meant he was not able to attack as he would have liked on the second.'

He had no such constraints on the second morning, his consistent pace ushering him into fourth place, ahead of Delecour. 'The handling of the car seems much better,' McRae said. 'I've got more confidence in the car and that has allowed me to push quite hard. We're really making improvements. I'm not having to fight the car to keep up the pressure.'

McRae illustrated that growing confidence – and no little courage – when he comprehensively outpaced his Championship rivals in torrential rain on the longest stage. A spin on the last stage of the leg possibly cost him third place but he was still within ten seconds of Sainz.

'It's been another good day,' McRae said. 'We managed to cut Carlos's advantage by almost ten seconds and if I hadn't spun on the last stage I think I would have gone in front of him. We had some really big moments in the rain. Any car on slick tyres and a dry set-up in those conditions is going to be really unpredictable and we had a couple of sideways incidents. It was more like driving on gravel than asphalt.'

McRae would have relished rain on the final day to accommodate his pursuit of the Citroëns but clear skies effectively left only third place in sight. McRae, as Sainz must have feared, chipped away the Toyota's advantage and began the final stage two tenths of a second ahead. To McRae's dismay, and under the scrutiny of the television cameras, a gear selection problem cost him crucial seconds and handed back that podium place to Sainz. Auriol, Mäkinen and Sainz claimed the controversial bonus points from the run.

'I went to change gear from third to second and the gear jammed in neutral,' McRae said. 'It was a very tight corner and with no control over the car we went into a half spin. I had to spin the car around before we could continue. We kept pushing hard to see if we could make up the time, or in case Carlos had a problem, but it wasn't to be. But overall it's been a good rally.'

Ford took advantage of the rule permitting retired drivers to return for the TV climax by entering Jean-Joseph and he posted tenth fastest time.

The top of the Drivers' Championship read: 1, Mäkinen 29 points; 2, Auriol 28 points; 3, McRae 23 points; 4, Sainz 21 points; 5, Bugalski 20 points.

Wilson reflects: 'When you consider that was our first proper asphalt rally finish, we had to be very happy with it. In reality [discounting the Citroëns] we finished second but we could have won. Colin said he missed a gear, but I think he probably tried a bit too hard as well. It was still a good performance, though.'

Produced, as it was, on tarmac, it appeared to add substance to the Championship challenge from McRae and Ford. The competition was tight, ripe for someone to exploit with a sudden surge. Mäkinen might do that, of course, but the Finn publicly recognised he suspected the push would come from McRae. The set swiftly changed back to gravel, and to Cordoba, Argentina. Surely the

Scotsman would excel. And this time those lightweights would not be in the way.

'I enjoy driving on gravel more than asphalt,' he said. 'And it's a good event. I enjoy the whole atmosphere. The rally has a reputation for being quite rough but I don't find the roads too bad. The surface is quite soft and sandy but there are a few rocks and boulders which can be damaging.'

Rådström was sufficiently recovered from his injury to reclaim his seat next to Gallagher. 'It's been hard just sitting and looking and listening, but I've been concentrating on my fitness and getting the strength back in my leg,' the Swede said. 'Over the past few weeks I've been counting down the days to the rally like a child counting down the school days before the summer holidays.'

His eagerness was apparent on the opening, super special stage, in which three cars competed simultaneously, to the frenzied approval of a 70,000 crowd. Rådström was fourth fastest, McRae sixth.

McRae opened up the Focus on the first orthodox stage, registering fastest time and sending out an ominous message to the rest. However, on the next test, the classic Giulio Cesare–Mina Clavero, he hit a huge rock, tipping the Focus on its side. McRae and Grist managed to haul the car back on to its wheels but the damage to the front suspension was too severe for them to continue.

'It's obviously disappointing,' McRae said. 'The car went really well on the first stage today and we set fastest time without pushing that hard. We were just unlucky to hit a rock but that's typical of Argentina. You have to pick your line very carefully and hope luck is on your side. It wasn't with us today.'

Rådström had better fortune, the tyre mousse counteracting a total of six punctures during the day. His consistency gave him sixth place overnight and he protected it for the rest of the rally. He lost visibility in a watersplash but the ever resourceful Gallagher wiped the windscreen clear and guided them home.

'It's superb for me to finish in the points,' Rådström said, 'after so long out of the driving seat. It will be a while before I can be a runner again but there's no problem driving.'

Wilson said: 'Thomas has driven exceptionally well here considering the circumstances. And it's his first appearance in Argentina. We'll go away with a lot of data which will put us in good stead for Greece, an event on which Thomas has competed before and one which Colin has won. So I think we have every reason to be confident there.'

The team were intent on reinforcing the Focus, in particular the suspension, in preparation for the Acropolis but Wilson maintains the car had no inherent weakness in Argentina.

'You have to put it into perspective,' he says. 'Colin hit a rock in Kenya and thought that was it, he was going home. He said if he'd hit a rock that big with the Subaru he would have retired. He just couldn't believe how strong the Focus was. So then he hits a rock in Argentina, different position, and it breaks a joint on the suspension. Thomas went round the whole rally and we never even changed the suspension pins. But as soon as that happened to Colin we were on the phone to do a complete redesign, and we had that redesign done and fitted to the cars for Greece.'

Juha Kankkunen's first Championship win in five years, achieved by overtaking a disgruntled Subaru team-mate Burns on the last stage, indicated an ever more open contest. Mäkinen now shared the title lead with Auriol, on 32 points, while McRae and Sainz were level on 23.

chapter six

Lap of the goddess

When they built the temple to the Goddess Athena, back in 447 to 432 BC, they can scarcely have imagined its mystical hold on charioteers approaching the third millennium AD. The spectre of the Parthenon, treasure of treasures on the most famous acropolis, pursues the modern chargers long after the ceremonial preliminaries of the fabled Greek event. There is no more awe-inspiring or symbolic landmark in the World Championship.

Drivers learn by chastening experience to be fatalistic yet here, more than almost anywhere, they surrender body and soul to the whim of a Higher Power. Reports from the recces up on the mountain stages, way beyond the stifling sprawl of the modern Athens, indicated the 1999 Acropolis Rally would be less forgiving than ever. Off-road vehicles had been hard-pressed to pick their way through the boulders and the ruts. Petter Solberg, sent on the recce to further his education, took 56 minutes to cover the 26km of the third stage. It was subsequently reduced to less than a third of its original length.

These were ominous warnings for Colin McRae and the Ford Martini team. The No. 1 driver had succumbed to a rocky trap in Argentina and any sense of foreboding would have been pardonable. He had won here twice before and the Focus was expected to excel on gravel. On these stages, however, 'gravel' appeared to be a wicked misnomer. Drivers encoun-

The Acropolis Rally is a rough and dusty ride.

tered stones as big as those much-photographed remnants of the Acropolis fortress. Malcolm Wilson's men reinforced the suspension of their car in readiness for the ordeal but acknowledged that nothing short of an armoured tank could guarantee survival.

Self-preservation was uppermost in McRae's mind as he prepared for this rally and the recce represented only a part of the strategic planning. The Scotsman and Nicky Grist, guided and cajoled by their trainer-physio, Alan Muckle, also took to their mountain bikes to hone physically and acclimatise for the event. They could anticipate ambient temperatures of more than 30°C and in-car temperatures perhaps twice as high.

'As long as you've done your training properly you shouldn't feel any more tired at the end of a day on the Acropolis than on any other rally,' McRae said. 'The important thing during the rally is to maintain the right level of fluid intake. Getting ready for a rally like this is the same for a driver as for the car. We test the Focus on rough roads and in the heat, and I train here in the days leading up to the rally to make sure I'm prepared as well as I can be. Although it's probably even hotter on the Safari, you don't drive flat out all the time there, so you get a breather. The Acropolis is more of a sprint event.'

Argentina may have dented McRae's Championship prospects but it served to bolster Thomas Rådström's aspirations in the other Focus. 'I've competed on this rally three times before and I know the terrain well,' the Swede said. 'We had a good drive in Argentina and the roads there were as rough as Greece in places. That was my first true gravel rally in the car and we got it to suit my driving style. I'm confident I can go well here. I'm looking forward to it.'

All the drivers had to look forward to

on the first day of the Acropolis Rally was a 2.4km super special stage – and the tedium of Athens' traffic. The irrelevance of the former and the mind-numbing frustration of the latter did nothing to enhance the case for these supposedly titillating show stages. Australia had championed the super special stage cause with a spectacular production, packaging a sample of the real thing with head to head combat for the benefit of arena spectators and a television audience. The super special held at Cordoba attracted a crowd of 70,000, seemingly endorsing the concept for those who believe rallying must market itself this way.

Tyre choice can be critical.

The purists – and those who contend rallying will be better served if it markets the genuine article – gleaned evidence in support of their case on this hot Sunday in Greece. A dust bowl obliterated the cars from view and rendered the exercise a farce. At least the Focus pair and the rest of the main contenders from an entry list of 114 came through unscathed. Of the locals probably only those heading to and from the beach will have found consolation in the congestion.

'Eight hours' effort for two minutes 16 seconds,' Guenther Steiner said disdainfully. 'What a waste of a day. The real rally starts tomorrow. The secret here is to know the limits of the engine and the transmission, and make sure you run as close to those limits as possible without crossing them. This event is definitely one of the toughest after the Safari and the most testing in Europe for the cars.'

The eight-hour round-trip brought the cars back along the coast road towards Corinth, to the new base for the rally, at the modest resort of Agaii Theodori. They were left in line in parc fermé and would be retrieved the following morning for serious business.

* * *

At 8am that Monday a vast gravel plateau greeted the cars and competitors of the Acropolis Rally. A neatly laid surface of grey-white stone had been provided for the first service point. This was an opportunity for the teams to make routine checks before sending the cars out on to the stage. Two canopies had been erected in front of a Ford truck and mechanics organised themselves for work. Malcolm Wilson scanned log sheets with his engineers and surveyed the scene with paternal care.

The tempo shifted up several gears the moment McRae's grunting No. 7 Focus turned into the Ford compound and parked beneath one of the canopies. McRae, dressed in blue bottoms and a white T-shirt, strolled towards the trestle table and took a plastic cup of tea. Such is the heat in the cars on this rally the drivers are allowed to dispense with the full fire-proof suit. As McRae chatted to Wilson's wife, Elaine, a dozen mechanics swarmed over his car. A particularly small mechanic climbed into the engine. A Michelin man – disappointingly slim – organised the removal of the wheels and tyres. The ten-minute operation was conducted calmly and methodically.

'We should be all right here,' Wilson said. 'Mind you, when you start to think like that you soon find out it's not. You tend to get a sharp reminder that you can never be sure of anything in rallying.'

Rådström's car, which arrived beneath the adjacent canopy, was subjected to the same ritual. Fred Gallagher, like Grist, went through the paperwork. Gallagher also munched his way through a banana.

'Who's on the windscreen?' Wilson wanted to know. Suddenly two mechanics appeared on the windscreen, then a third, armed with spray and rolls of paper. The wheels were gunned back on, the engine man extricated himself, doors were closed and Rådström, too, was on his way to the first meaningful stage of the rally. The crews packed their gear and headed north-west to a service park where they were due to meet up with their rally cars again after the morning's second stage.

Wilson and the higher command climbed into their Ford Galaxy, code-named Super 1, and took Highway 8 towards Athina, hoping both his rally cars would survive what he reckoned were two of the toughest stages in the entire Championship. Gallagher predicted casualties. Everyone hoped McRae would curb his natural instincts, but then it was generally acknowledged he had long since outgrown his youthful exuberance. The relatively smooth motorway ride, the profusion of colourful flower bushes and the still sea were equally comforting.

Radio messages, bouncing off an aircraft somewhere overhead, kept drivers and team in contact. McRae had a query about an ignition light but was assured he had no problem. Grist relayed their stage time and John Millington, the co-ordination manager, riding in Super 1, kept the Welshman informed of their opponents' progress: Didier, Carlos, Juha. Colin was quickest.

The support vehicles were now climbing and the landscape was changing dramati-

Rådström briefly leads the way.

cally. You could begin to imagine the test confronting the competitors and their snarling hi-tech beasts. And yet here, along this winding road, nature and man were in tranquil harmony: pines and olive groves, goatherds and peasant farmers. If the juxtaposition seemed remarkable to anyone they were too preoccupied to say. They had word that Burns might have gearbox problems, and that Gronholm had engine trouble. Road cars were racing to viewing points on one of the later stages. The Ford Martini convoy turned off towards the service park.

The mechanics are incredible – they do a lot in a 20-minute service stop

Again the incongruity was stark: an instant village of gaudily painted motorhomes and trucks, even helicopters, alongside primitive homesteads and smallholdings. The Ford motorhome is run by Stuart and Di Spires, veteran caterers and confidants of the Formula One circuit. With them were their regular Grand Prix colleagues, Graham and Tracey Ogden, as well as Pamela Brise, of M-Sport. They have the task of feeding, watering and, if necessary, consoling the team through the World Rally Championship.

Vans laden with tyres, parts and tools, and equipped with work benches and lathes, were parked at right angles to the blue bus, forming a private compound. A blue rope extended across the open side to prevent spectators from encroaching on the central area, where blue plastic groundsheets and canopies had been positioned in readiness for the cars. Another blue rope separated the workplace from the motorhome hospitality area. The mechanics would have 20 minutes to work on each car, and they can get through a lot of work in 20 minutes. In Kenya they changed a gearbox, driveshaft, dampers and springs, and rear differential in one 20-minute stop.

'These lads are incredible,' Graham Ogden said. 'F1 lads will tinker all afternoon on their cars inside a nice clean garage, but these lads will rip a car apart and put it together again at service parks in all sorts of conditions. It's hot and dusty here, but in Sweden they've got the snow and ice to contend with, and in such as Britain it's usually wet, muddy and cold. But no matter what the weather's like they throw themselves on the floor and under the car and just get on with it.

'You have to be prepared to be more fluid in rallying. In Formula One everything is in position and set to an exact schedule. Here it can change so quickly. You can plan one thing and find yourself having to do another. The people are much more relaxed. They'll come over from other teams and talk. It's very professional and serious, but not so intense that they can't enjoy it.'

The team were enjoying this. They heard that McRae, despite clipping a stone on the last stage, had no serious problem and was second overall. The news on Rådström was better still. He had gone into the lead.

Martin Whitaker, making a flying visit to the rally, arrived just in time to join Wilson and Steiner in the reception committee for McRae, the Focus materialising from a cloud of dust. In a moment the car was jacked up, its wheels removed and every orifice opened. The activity was more feverish this time, but still controlled. A TV camera crew closed in on McRae, empty drink bottle in hand, as he talked to Steiner. The battle-scarred undertray of the Focus provided another close-up. An FIA official was also keen to take a look. Another heavyweight team huddle completed proceedings and the McRae-Grist car was sent on its way.

Rådström, in compliance with the official rally scheduling, ran behind McRae. He was still limping, the legacy of his broken leg, but was palpably unrestrained in the car. The completion of his service gave the crew a break to eat and rest. Rådström's parents were already savouring the pasta.

One facility conspicuously absent was a

The dust trail and helicopter chart McRae's course.

toilet. There was one in the motorhome, of course, but access to that had to be limited. Running water was a luxury not available out here, and this was a team of 40-plus – as well as guests. 'The lads just go somewhere round the back of the bus,' said a droll Stuart Spires. 'All part of the joys of rallying.'

The team feared a leak of a different kind when Gallagher reported a power steering problem, then a brake problem. The drivers and co-drivers were on their own for these three midday stages. They were allowed advice but no hands-on assistance before the next service. Millington handed over to Martin Wilkinson, project controller, who in an equally calm manner told Gallagher to check the fluid level and where to find replenishment.

We've come a long way in a short time – now there's a lot of pressure

Listening anxiously out on a rocky thistle-lined road, were Whitaker, Elaine Wilson, Sharon Grist and a number of guests. They could testify to the severity of the terrain. One of their hire cars had a puncture. Elaine and Sharon had to get out and push. They never made it to the stage. All they saw was a distant dust trail.

It couldn't have been Rådström. Gallagher radioed the message they had stopped. 'There was a hell of a noise ... a hell of a vibration ... I think it's a piston ... there's a hole.'

Grist reported he and McRae were through OK. They had passed a stricken Auriol on the stage. The team told Grist and McRae of their team-mates' plight. The rally was over for Rådström and Gallagher, and now their crew were trying to organise an airlift from the stage. Just like those thistles, the magnificent scenery had a pernicious sting. The team informed assembling journalists that the No. 8 Focus ran over a rock which holed the sump, triggering a succession of faults that eventually brought the car to a halt.

Some of Rådström's mechanics were also making arrangements for an early retreat. As we heard, this is a fluid business. Other mechanics were reinforcing an undertray for McRae, the lesson of Rådström's demise taken on board. 'They used one of my lasagne pans to do that on the Monte Carlo,' Di Spires said. 'They were desperate for some metal and that was the best we could come up with. But it did the trick.'

Another alarm might have demanded similarly drastic action. Jimmy McRae's gravel car, a white Escort Cosworth with extended headlights like frog's eyes, parked behind the bus, rolled forward into a scooter, the impact setting off the alarm. A red-faced Jimmy was summoned to confront an unsmiling scooter owner, much to the amusement of the Ford camp.

The light relief was perfectly timed. Rådström's retirement was a setback, even if rallying folk have learned to be philosophical. Hazard of the job. McRae was still in, although the word went round the huge park he had dropped a place. Whitaker told a TV interviewer: 'Of course the Championship is a realistic objective for us.'

Wilson was sitting at one of the tables, under an umbrella, eating lunch with his wife. It was a time for quiet reflection.

'This is a pity because Thomas was going well, but it's the sort of thing you have to cope with in rallying,' Wilson said. 'Colin's looking pretty good and we've got to put everything behind him now. Before the season started nobody expected us to be in this situation. We've come a long way in a short time. Now there's pressure, a lot of pressure. That's something else we've got to handle.'

At 1.57pm McRae came in for his service and by now a small and enthusiastic crowd had gathered at the blue rope. They watched the team leap into their perfectly choreographed routine. Rådström's canopy and sheet had already been put away. The catering crew were clearing the hospitality area. They had to move back down to the coast for the last service of the day. McRae stepped inside the air-conditioned bus to escape the heat and attention. At 2.16pm Grist called up into the bus: 'OK, Col.' Seconds later McRae ran out, jumped into the car and pulled away.

Whitaker was also on his way. Ford had a major announcement to make later in the week. They had bought Jackie Stewart's Formula One team. The tyre boys on the Acropolis Rally had pressing business of their own. It took four of them to push the laden tyre trolley across rough gravel to the ramp at the back of the truck. And the team still had to rescue Rådström and Gallagher from the wilderness. A helicopter crew reported no sighting of them so a car was sent to the stage. All of which conjured a picture of the pair sitting in the shade of a fig tree somewhere, whiling away the time. Unfortunately for them, the fruit was not yet ripe. Then came word they were being brought out of the stage in a minibus, with the car in tow.

The ever-composed Millington, content Rådström and Gallagher were in safe hands, switched his attention to the remaining Focus as Super 1 and other support vehicles took the twisting, plunging road through the bleached rocks. Grist reported good progress on the stage. 'Well done, Nicky,' Millington replied.

McRae negotiated the final stage of the day with no apparent drama. In fact, Carlos Sainz smilingly suggested to the Ford team their man was taking it easy. The Spaniard patently was. Tactics had come into play here. No-one was eager to be first on the road the following day to act as sweeper for the rest. McRae clocked off in second place, behind Burns's Subaru.

McRae, still sitting in his car, opened the door and gave his thoughts to a small, crouching group of British pressmen: 'It's rougher than I expected, even after the recce. You can't go 100 per cent all the time. It's a case of backing off when you know you have to. We're in a good position. There could be a lot more changes tomorrow. I'm going for the win. I need to for the Championship. But at the same time I'm not going to throw it all away. If I can't win then I'll get the best result possible.

'I'm happy with the suspension. It's stronger here. I don't know what went wrong with Thomas yet but you can't let that affect you. You have to do your own thing. You know these things can happen, especially when the stages are as rough as these.'

Grist completed the checking-in formalities with the controllers and McRae drove the car the short distance to the final service point. A helicopter landed close by, yards from a humble single-storey house. It could be safely assumed the householder and his wife weren't about to step out with their weekly shopping.

As the Ford crew attacked the car again, Grist appeared to be working through his shopping list, clipped to a board. A TV reporter stopped him long enough for a

Dreaming of the Championship?

brief interview. 'No complaints today,' the Welshman said. 'We're feeling our way. No dramas. Our top speed was 186kph. People don't do that on the motorway. Last year we were second at this point and remember where we finished? First. We're OK.'

Wilson straightened the blue plastic groundsheet as his mechanics took a hammer to the car, reinforcing the area around the wheel arch. With all the technology available to them these days, it is reassuring to know the old skills have not disappeared.

Grist, meanwhile, was facing another camera. 'I don't have to tell Colin what to do. He's the best driver, he's very professional. Tomorrow is the longest day and we'll maybe need a bit of caution. It'll only get a bit easier on the last day. The rocks and dust are problems. So is the heat. It's 65°C and more in the car. It's like a sauna. But that's all part of it. We're used to it.'

I don't tell Colin what to do – he's the best driver, very professional

Wilson was down on his haunches, supervising more work on an undertray, as McRae, gnawing at a chocolate bar, was presented for the TV cameras. It was put to him there was a case for taking time penalties deliberately to drop down the order, but he said he did not think that tactic had been on the agenda. 'It's still wide open. Hopefully it will be close again tomorrow night and then I can go for it on the last day.'

McRae climbed into his rally car for the final time that day and headed for parc fermé. From there he would go to the team hotel and join his wife, Alison, and their six-month-old daughter, Hollie. Muckle would give him a once-over and massage and, after dinner, McRae would endeavour to get an early night in readiness for the longest day.

Back at the service park it was Wilson's turn to face the cameras. 'Colin drove very sensibly today. The only stage where he really pushed was the first one. You don't really want to be first on the road tomorrow. Ideally you'd like to be fourth on the road. Carlos was certainly slowing up this afternoon. The first stage tomorrow is very fast, one of the smoothest in Europe. It's a very important stage. Last year Colin was second on the road and fastest on that stage. He's up for it.

'His car has taken a real battering today but everything is OK. It's just a case of making the usual changes: suspension, gearbox and so on. Thomas wasn't so lucky. He cracked the sump and the oil leaked away. A typical Acropolis day, really. There's still a great unknown about Greece. A bit like the Safari. There's no way you can predict a winner. We just hope to get a clear run and that the tyres are all right.'

The day had taken its toll on Graham Ogden, who flopped in the shade at the back of the service truck. The elevation of the park gave him the benefit of a refreshing sea breeze, which wafted over him. The temperature inside the mobile kitchen was probably even higher than that in the rally car. 'It's a classic case of dehydration,' Muckle said.

There would be even more heat on McRae the following day. News was filtering through that Burns had clocked in three minutes late, so incurring a 30-second penalty and dropping down to fourth. The revised order was: 1, McRae; 2, Mäkinen; 3, Sainz; 4, Burns; 5, Loix; 6, Kankkunen.

'He's very brave,' Wilson said of Burns. Just like the market traders lining the main street of Agii Theodori, the English driver had set his stall out.

* * *

Crews and the rally's accompanying entourage were stirring before the sun that Tuesday morning. Muckle woke up the drivers at 5 o'clock. By then Jimmy McRae was already at work in the gravel car and doubtless making little effort to stop the Escort fishtailing. Colin needed all the help he could muster at the head of the field.

Some of those following the rally to the

northerly mountains on this second leg opted for a more leisurely route, crossing the bay by ferry and watching the sun rise over docile water. Villages and beaches at the far side were unspoiled by the commercialism grinding its relentless course nearer Athens. The beckoning climb was spectacular. Was that really snow on the distant peaks? More unlikely white stuff formed a welcome, cooling cloud cover.

Lorries pounded a red-brown trail from the bauxite mines, providing an indication of the first stage faced by the drivers that morning. McRae's necessary caution toppled him from the leading position, while Burns instantly compensated for the overnight penalty to reclaim the advantage. A tortoise on the road to the next stage was palpably unmoved. Were the beehives warning of more stings to come?

The sun had bullied its way through the clouds but at this altitude it was less potent and the air fresher. The scenery was stunning. A group of about 30 people, mainly photographers, had positioned themselves on the outside of a rising left-hand sweep. Behind them, an endless drop. The FIA safety helicopter swooped across the valley and a voice on the loud-hailer instructed the stragglers still wandering along the white, stony track to get their butts in gear.

Minutes later the course car ploughed through, spraying those on the outside with bullets of rock and leaving in its wake a curtain of dust. The flinching group turned back and an excited buzz replaced the noise of growling engine. The mix of languages reflected the international field: Italian, English, French, Spanish, even Greek.

Then, the grunt of another car, the Ford Focus, from the distant mountainside, the dust rising from the trees and tracing its path. For perhaps half a minute the grunt, and the dust, receded. Silence

'Are you sure about this Nicky?'

returned, apart, that is, from the persistent whirr of the chopper's blades. Suddenly dust appeared from the trees again. This time the grunt was louder, and becoming louder still. It was more menacing, and spluttering inelegantly as Grist called the corners and McRae punched the gears. All the tension, the eager anticipation, passed in a moment as the Focus, hugging the inside, its back-end hanging out at roughly 30°, exploded by. Even the dayglo red was indecipherable in the fury of stones and dust. McRae's front left wheel ran barely a couple of inches from a spectator crouched at the foot of the inside bank. He appeared not to bat an eyelid. Perhaps it all happened so quickly he was oblivious to the proximity of the Focus and the potential danger. The gasps and nervous laughter from the other side of the road provided a starkly contrasting reaction. Standing there in the firing line, they seemed strangely masochistic volunteers for death row.

The service area had the colour, clamour and urgency of a market place

They braced themselves again, this time for Mäkinen's Mitsubishi. Cameras were cocked and clicking until the Finn was within feet of them. Then they spun and cowered, leaving their backs exposed to the chippings and dust. A TV man, obviously a veteran of these assignments, was equipped with duster for his lens and smog mask for his mouth and nose. He even removed a particularly lethal-looking rock from the middle of the road. Kankkunen took a noticeably central line. Just as well that cameraman smoothed his way for him.

Soon the gallery began to drift away. The top drivers had gone through and the rest of the field would see more retreating figures. Or none at all. It is the same for the amateur enthusiasts the world over and a wonder they are not terminally dispirited. A ripple of applause at the crest gave encouragement to at least one local, but then he was running in the top 20. According to someone at the side of the road, McRae was down to fifth, paying the price for clearing away substantially more than the cameraman could have managed.

Down in the service area – another spacious, dusty site – the temperature was considerably higher. It was busier than the main park used the day before. It had the colour, clamour and urgency of a market place. And yet it was still orderly, never manic. Wilson's bowl of pasta fell neatly into its time slot.

'It looks as though Subaru did the right thing,' he conceded. 'I'm sure the tyres have a lot to do with it. Seat's form would seem to confirm that. But Colin will chip away and if he's there or thereabouts tomorrow he can win it. I don't fear anyone. If anyone can do it in a situation like this, Colin can. The car has taken a pounding bodily but it's OK. The problem we have is that it's still 30 kilos overweight and if the tyres are not at their optimum, that weight can make a big difference. We're working on that, of course, but as always it's a question of time and money.'

McRae did, indeed, make up time in the middle of the day and warm applause from spectators behind the rope welcomed him back to his crew. He climbed from his car to be handed a cold, wet towel, which he gratefully draped over his head. He had a word with Wilson and his engineers before turning to the sanctuary of the bus. Grist, into his ritual of perpetual motion, was stopped in his tracks when Dr Ravin Naik handed him a towel and urged him to use it. Those who know Grist said he had never looked so exhausted. Graham Ogden, still suffering the effects of the previous day's heat, stayed back at the hotel, nursed by his wife.

Wilson joined the workers on McRae's car, the dust seemingly baked on, presumably after plunging into a water splash. Martin Wilkinson rushed over to the bus and asked Stuart Spires if he could spare any water. 'Ten minutes, lads,' Wilkinson called out.

Wilson, now one of the lads, had a

spray in one hand, cloth in the other. Philip Baker and Duncan Gallagher temporarily abandoned their marketing and Press relations duties to help the clean up. At last the names of McRae and Grist, along with the Cross of St Andrew and the Welsh Dragon, became visible. So, too, the colours of Martini. Presentation is important. McRae took another gulp from a bottle and reversed from beneath the canopy. Simultaneously, Stuart Spires was taking down the umbrellas. He and Di had to return to the service park at Agii Theodori. Pamela would take a bootload of sandwiches and other provisions to the afternoon service.

There was a discernible new step in the team. McRae had planned an attack late in the day and there was talk that the times of the first stage might be scrapped because of a mix-up by the organisers, who sent out cars at three-minute intervals instead of two. That proved fanciful speculation but McRae's optimism was genuine.

Super 1 was on the road again and heard from the No. 7 Focus that they were through stage 13. However, McRae reported a misfire and high temperatures. He was asked if they would be able to change the plugs. No problem, they replied. McRae and Grist stopped on the road and although Super 1 also pulled up, the drivers were permitted no physical assistance. They willingly conceded they had the benefit of divine intervention on the following mountain stage. The Focus came over the crest, flat in sixth, and dropped a wheel into a ditch. As driver and co-driver held their breath, contemplating an unscheduled, rapid and painful descent, they were pitched back on to the road and resumed their favoured course.

At the service park, team members had to retrieve umbrellas scattered by arriving helicopters. The tyre men moved smartly, too, reacting to McRae's requirements for the next stage. The activity was even more frenetic when the rally car came in. McRae buried his head in another wet towel and peeled a banana as the crew hammered and tugged at the Focus. Wilson pulled on the driver's door, which had been damaged in that near miss. They told themselves this had been a good omen. They were unlucky in Argentina.

The ever calm and orderly John Millington consults with an attentive Gallagher.

Here they had got away with it. There was a slight concern about the gearbox. Third had been a little uncooperative. But with only two stages to negotiate before the overnight halt, they felt there was no serious threat. They were fourth and in touch for the big push on the final day.

Three kilometres into that penultimate stage of Tuesday, Grist solemnly informed the team: 'It keeps jumping out of gear. All we can get is first.'

Millington, the tone of his voice never wavering from its calm, business-like pitch, told Grist to make contact again at the end of the stage. McRae communicated the next resigned message: 'We've got no drive ... only first ... The gears are completely knackered ... Can you send us a car, please?'

Super 1 acknowledged and then sent out its own message: 'All mobiles be aware, Colin has retired. Colin has retired.'

With a long road section, as well as another stage, ahead McRae had no option. For the Ford Martini team, the Acropolis Rally was over with more than a day remaining. McRae's car was towed to its final service area and relieved of its broken gearbox. Muckle retrieved Grist's drink bladder. As engineers examined the gearbox inside a truck, Wilson studied onboard TV footage of his drivers' escape on the mountainside. Pictures showed the road ahead, then the sky, and then the road again. All, it seemed, in a mesmerising instant.

Wilson admits the heat is on.

The mood, although by no means frivolous, was far from funereal. Breakdowns come with the territory. The team still had work to do and they set about it without any apparent weeping and gnashing of teeth. Some of them would be flying back a day earlier than planned to start on the programme leading up to the next rally.

'I feel for Colin, the way he's driven today,' Wilson said. 'He might not have been able to win but he would definitely have been on for second. We'll have a good look at the transmission and then try to make sure we don't have this problem again. The trouble is that once you lose a gear the whole thing can go because these sequential gearboxes are so sensitive. Every rally is different, bringing different challenges and problems.'

Wilson shared that philosophical viewpoint with the usual coterie of TV reporters. A few yards away a British newspaper reporter dictated his story on a mobile phone. It told of Richard Burns's charge to the verge of victory, and of McRae's misfortune. As Wilson drove away, the sight of local amateurs, stretching their meagre resources to prepare for the final day, must have compounded his dismay.

Early that evening McRae and Grist changed into their civvies, sat with their wives, baby Hollie and a few friends at the beach bar of their hotel. The setting sun and the benign sea proffered a soothing embrace. The beers probably had the same effect.

'It's really disappointing because the stages remaining had all been used yesterday, so they would have been relatively clear and I think we could have won,' McRae said quietly. 'I would certainly have had a go, anyway. This obviously makes it difficult for the Championship but at least if Richard wins, it will keep things pretty open. Maybe things will go our way for the rest of the season.'

Grist was grateful just to be sitting there. 'The accident we could have had today would have been pretty nasty,' he said. 'It was a bit of a drop down into the valley below. Not vertical, but when you're barrel-rolling you don't stop easily. It was a six left over a jump. We approached it at full speed and jumped a lot further than Colin expected. Obviously you don't do the notes in a rally car. We landed on the edge of the road, sideways, with the back wheel down over the bank, and a big lump of I don't know what did a lot of damage to Colin's side. I expected us to barrel-roll sideways down to the bottom of the hill but it kicked us back on the road and fortunately we were able to carry on.

'Our luck ran out on the next stage. I don't think that off could have affected the gearbox. We've had it jump out of gear a few times today and everybody thought it would get through. But then it spat out of gear, put it back, spat it out again. We went round a couple of corners, round a hairpin left, accelerated up a hill. It spat it out, put it in, spat it out, and that was it. Couldn't get any gear at all. Just first gear in the end, so you've got no chance.

'When you've put so much effort in it's a feeling of bitter disappointment, because we're trying to fight for the Championship. I think we were a little spoiled in the early part of the season. No-one expected such a good start as that. But now we're beginning to wonder. We've had four retirements and that's a lot to make up. Unless we have a real winning streak over the next few I think it's going to be quite difficult. I wouldn't say it's impossible, though, because generally Colin does come strong towards the end of the year and it's still very open. It's a case of developing the car and making it strong enough for Colin to drive it as quickly as he can.'

I expected us to barrel-roll down to the bottom of the valley

Before all that Grist and his wife were looking forward to spending a couple of days along the coast, while the McRaes were relishing the prospect of returning to Scotland for a break.

At five o'clock the following morning Steiner and some of his staff were checking in at Athens airport. They were back at base long before Burns, his path made easier by his team's rock-clearing operation, was confirmed as winner of the 1999 Acropolis Rally. Sainz was second, Mäkinen third. Mäkinen now led the Championship with 36 points, followed by Auriol on 32, Sainz on 29, and McRae and Burns on 23.

chapter seven

Teamwork

Colin McRae and the rest of the drivers and co-drivers, the men in the front line, rightly take the limelight, the plaudits and, indeed, the flak according to their performance. Rallying is generally perceived as a sport for individuals, or at most pairs, rather than a team game, and ultimately the result does rest in the hands of those in the car. However, like Formula One and other forms of motor racing, rallying owes as much to teamwork, tactics, planning, understanding, trust, complementary skills, strength in depth, selfless commitment, following up, tracking back, filling in, overlapping, covering and supporting as football, cricket, rugby or any other readily recognisable team sport. A glimpse behind the scenes at a World Rally Championship event presents irrefutable evidence.

The Ford Martini team, directed by Malcolm Wilson, is more than 40 strong on the road, and even that represents only a portion of the manpower channelled into the effort. By the end of 2000 Wilson expects the workforce at M-Sport to number 150. And then you have the Ford technicians in Britain and Germany who have made vital contributions to the creation and development of the Focus and its myriad components.

Organisation, structure, expertise, dedication, enthusiasm, strong nerves and cool heads are just a few of the essentials in the creation and moulding of a successful rally team. Equally important are flexibility, a willingness to work long, even insane hours, in ever changing environments, climates and conditions. To the adventurer and rally fan the prospect might seem idyllic, and few here would swap their jobs for a pigeonhole in the real world. But this is no paid holiday, and much as the mechanics appreciate the opportunity to travel across Europe, to Australia, New Zealand, Argentina, Kenya and China, the view underneath a rally car rarely changes.

The Ford team travel in a fleet of vehicles and set up camp at the designated service parks, where the mechanics and engineers work on the rally cars in the allotted time. They have their own caterers, who ensure a constant supply of sustenance, a doctor and a physio. Usually first on the road are the gravel crews, who make a final check on the stages before the competitors go through.

Malcolm Wilson oversees the job on the rally just as he does back at the workshop in his beloved Cumbria. The chain of command is defined yet never obviously elitist. Wilson and his lieutenants are prepared to pitch in with the rank and file in the heat of battle. Everyone here has to be a team player, regardless of his official role or title. If they were not they would be exposed and discarded. Here are just a few of those players, a cross-section of the Ford Martini rally team and their thoughts on the common cause:

Guenther Steiner, Project Leader

It helps to have a liking and instinct for rally driving when you come from that part of northern Italy which merges into what is effectively a mountain state. In many respects Steiner has the characteristics, as well as the name, you might expect to find over the border in Austria. His role demands a cool, orderly mind, the capacity to anticipate and the nerve to pursue. And yet he has the ready smile and personal touch of a Latin. He appears equally comfortable with his peers and his staff.

That seemingly perfect blend for leadership and man-management is as important out in the field as it is back in the workshop and drawing office. Having put together the team which designed and nurtured the Focus rally car, he is constantly monitoring and reviewing his development strategy, and on the event his very presence is a fortifying and assuring pillar.

'My main responsibility is general organisation, liaising and finding new ideas,' he said. 'Once the season starts the schedule is so busy, rally after rally, and of course with the Focus we are still developing the car because there is much more potential. It is difficult to say how much, but for sure there is more. The problem is time.

'I do look at the other cars but I am not one of those who likes to copy. I am sure others are copying us because in rallying it's not like a racing formula where you can hide something. Everything for the prototype was confidential and that part of the operation worked well. But of course it was a very tight schedule. The first people were signed up in January and we moved to Millbrook on 1 February. I employed around eight people at the start of the project and a lot didn't join us before March.

'It was a very tight schedule and now,

The Ford Martini team set up camp in Sweden.

looking back, you can say we needed more time, but there was no point in thinking about that then. We had to do it. And it was all new, not just the technical side. We were building up relationships as well as a workshop and the car. Nothing was there. That was the biggest thing. But it worked out all right.

'My advantage was that I knew what we had to do. We did everything from new. You could take the best parts of the earlier car but as soon as you do that you compromise, you work around things. Maybe it wasn't right to start with but at least you have the scope to develop it. If you take something that is already there, let's say an upright, and it is developed to the end, there is no scope any more. After seven years a part should be at the end of its development. There is nothing more you can do with it.

The people involved drive the project – they are the heartbeat

'So this was our strategy, to have something new, knowing we could always develop and improve it. And so it is interesting that now everybody is beginning to copy us a bit. All the cars are beginning to show that, they all become similar. That is normal.'

The creation of a rally car is essentially a technical and engineering exercise, and the organisation of the team and Championship programme a logistical and strategic operation. A cold detachment might serve to enhance the project, but scientific achievement is ultimately measured in human emotion and rallying provides glorious proof. The people involved drive the concept. They are the heartbeat. They take the stress and savour the accomplishment.

'It does become an emotional thing because for four months you see nothing and then suddenly it takes shape and it's such a good feeling,' Steiner said, his eyes ablaze. 'When things are behind schedule you get anxious. You think, "Oh no, two weeks late." And of course the closer you get to the start of the season there is more and more pressure, because everybody is asking about it. "How's it going?" In the beginning they ask every month, then every week, and at the end it's every day.

'You feel good and relieved when the car runs for the first time, and yet you know there is still the testing to come, and then the first rally before you can be sure how good it is. We thought it would be good but you can never be certain. You cannot be absolutely confident because it is hard to compare cars in rallying. It's not like a circuit, where you take a time and you know where you are. You can go on a stage and take a time, but there are so many different things to consider: the road conditions, the tyres and so on.

'For me the really good feeling was at Monte Carlo, where we were fast straightaway. That was when we were able to say, "We haven't been wrong here." That was actually more exciting than the first run with the car, to see it in competition, where you really know for the first time.'

The emotions were stretched in the opposite direction over the issue of the water pump and Steiner shared the burden.

'There was a feeling of anger and for me responsibility also. There was a lot of discussion and I took over the liaison with the FIA. We were led to believe it was OK but now, with hindsight, I think we should have seen a possible problem. What really annoyed me was the story that the FIA were helping us. That was not correct. As Martin Whitaker said, the only thing we could do then was to go and show them. And that's what we did. We had ten days to do it and we got it done.'

The relief and elation gathered a momentum all of its own and Steiner found himself steering a possible Championship campaign a year ahead of schedule. The Focus was exceeding first season expectations and McRae was reaping the benefits of his technical input as well as his driving talent.

'Colin has given us good feedback all the way through, and that was especially important at the beginning. We had to get the guidance on where we were and he was fantastic for that. He has done this for many years now and he understands rally cars. He tries to do everything quick, quick. And correctly. He is demanding but that is what you need. It's no good if the driver is not professional.

'He is a strong driver and he drives the team, and that is good. The team know he is good so they have confidence in him. Other drivers might have to prove themselves to win that confidence, but Colin has proved himself already. He is also cool and quite relaxed about everything. If you compare this with Formula One, he is the same as Schumacher or Senna. He has that little bit more than the others. I don't know where it comes from but he has it. As a driver he is absolutely the best.

'Of course, when he won in Safari, and then in Portugal, we realised we could try to win the Drivers' World Championship in 1999. But we had to win more events and we still had some teething problems with the car. You have to sort these out so that when you get to the service on a rally you don't lose too much time. We are not late, but sometimes it is tight. We are still learning. It is a new car and we don't have time to go testing every day. So you do what you can this year, and then go on to next year.'

Martin Wilkinson, Event Controller

On the shop floor, be it in the factory or at the event, Wilkinson is closer to the focal point of the job. He is hands-on, ensuring the general concept is followed through in detail, that the operation runs smoothly and on time.

'In the workshop I control the quality of the car build. Not the spec of the car, the engineers do that. I control how things are built in to the car, the general appearance, and also any special parts we may need. I fly out to an event a day before the others and link up with the lads who drive out, set up the workshop area, check out the vans, and do any final jobs we need to do on the rally cars so that when the guys come out they know everything's under control and they can get

Steiner lends a sympathetic ear as Rådström makes a point, watched by Wilson and his fan club.

straight down to it. I'm in control of the cars till they go to the start of the rally, to parc fermé. I control Colin's car and somebody does a similar job on the second car. That means organising the boys, letting them know what we're going to be doing, who's going to do what.'

Wilkinson, from Carlisle, joined Wilson's team when they were awarded the Ford contract. Rallying is not only his work, it is also his passion. He is typical of the workforce.

'My father was a rallying fanatic, so I've always been to rallying. My cousin used to be into racing but I always preferred rallying to racing. I've done a bit and used to fancy taking it up more seriously but not now. When we finish building the cars I shake them down so I do get to drive them. I suppose that's my way of getting any frustrations out of me. You're bound to think it would have been good to compete when you get your hands on something like this car. It's a fantastic car to drive. You have to drive it a lot to be able to understand just how good it is, and how well Colin drives it.

He is demanding but that's fine – if the car's not perfect he can't drive perfectly

'He's just got something special about him. There's no other driver in the world as good. I think it's his sheer courage and determination. And he's just so skilled. He's a natural driver. He doesn't have to work at it. The likes of Carlos have to work hard at it. And Colin can just turn on the speed when he really needs to. Maybe it's that he can push himself over the limit and stay there. He is demanding but that's no problem for us because we know he's trying to get everything perfect. If the car isn't perfect you can't expect him to go out and drive perfectly.'

Perfection is an even more elusive target once a rally is underway. McRae and the other drivers often return their cars to service in dire need of surgery.

'On the event most of the problems are purely damage to the car. Especially somewhere like the Safari and the Acropolis. I assess whether or not we have time to fix it, and whether or not it is safe to continue as it is or whether we should perhaps take some time penalties and try to repair the car properly. It's a matter of sorting out what parts to change, where and when. I get a list from the engineers of what they would like to change and then see what the cars are like when they come in. If we don't want to take penalties I keep an eye on the time and make sure the car goes out on time.

'There are times when you feel down, when the conditions are tough and things are not going right. If I said there weren't I'd be a fool. But the good times always outweigh the bad ones. There's rarely any bother or cross words. Most of the guys are great and they work well together. You have to. Part of my job is to keep them calm and relaxed, and if you can do that you'll get through the difficult times. It's the same if the drivers have problems between services. I'll get on the radio to them and talk them through it. There's no point at all in getting excited because that will transmit through to the drivers. If you're panicking they are going to detect that.

'It's good to be able to relax a bit if you can in the evenings. The lads will have a couple of beers and a quiet meal. If we finish early enough we might even go for a swim. Many times, though, we get late nights preparing for the rally. Monte Carlo, for instance, we worked through the night there. It was a tight schedule and we were trying to make sure everything was right. I know we had a problem there but the result justified all the hard work. Same before Sweden and again on the Safari. Sometimes it's hard to keep up your enthusiasm when it's three or four in the morning and you know you should have been in bed hours before.

'You don't get anybody here who's bigheaded or anything like that. Nobody thinks they're better than anybody else. I don't know how our wages compare with Formula One but I'm sure that if you were to offer the boys another few thousand pounds a year they wouldn't say "No." I don't think money is much of an issue, though. They're motivated enough.'

That motivation can, inevitably, be tested by the dual responsibilities of professional and private life. Wilkinson, 28, is married and has a young son.

'Of course, it's very hard when you're a family man,' he said. 'Anybody who says it's not is not telling the truth. I'm quite fortunate because my wife used to compete in rallies, so she's probably more understanding than most. I'm one of only a few who do every event. I daren't work out how many days of the year I'm away from home.

'It's quite a small world, the Championship scene. It's close-knit. We often stay in the same hotels as other teams, and mechanics do move from team to team, so you're always seeing old friends and colleagues. Every now and then you'll offer to help the lads at another team because you never know when you might need some help. We wouldn't go and help them work on the car, but if they were short of something, if they wanted some bolts or whatever, then we'd help out as far as we could there. If you don't get that in Formula One then there's the difference. It's a lot more friendly.

'A few of the lads here have been in racing and say they prefer rallying. They like the atmosphere here. The other difference is that when you go to a race you're there for the full weekend, in the one place, with the same routine, and there's no change. Whereas in rallying we can be in the middle of the countryside, move from place to place, with everything we need. Plus, the cars aren't going round the same circuit all the time.

'I have thought about what I might do in the future but I haven't come to any conclusions yet. I'll stick it out as long as I enjoy it. If you're ambitious you're bound to want to look towards management. But I still love to be involved directly with the cars. I wouldn't want to go too much higher and not be involved with the cars.'

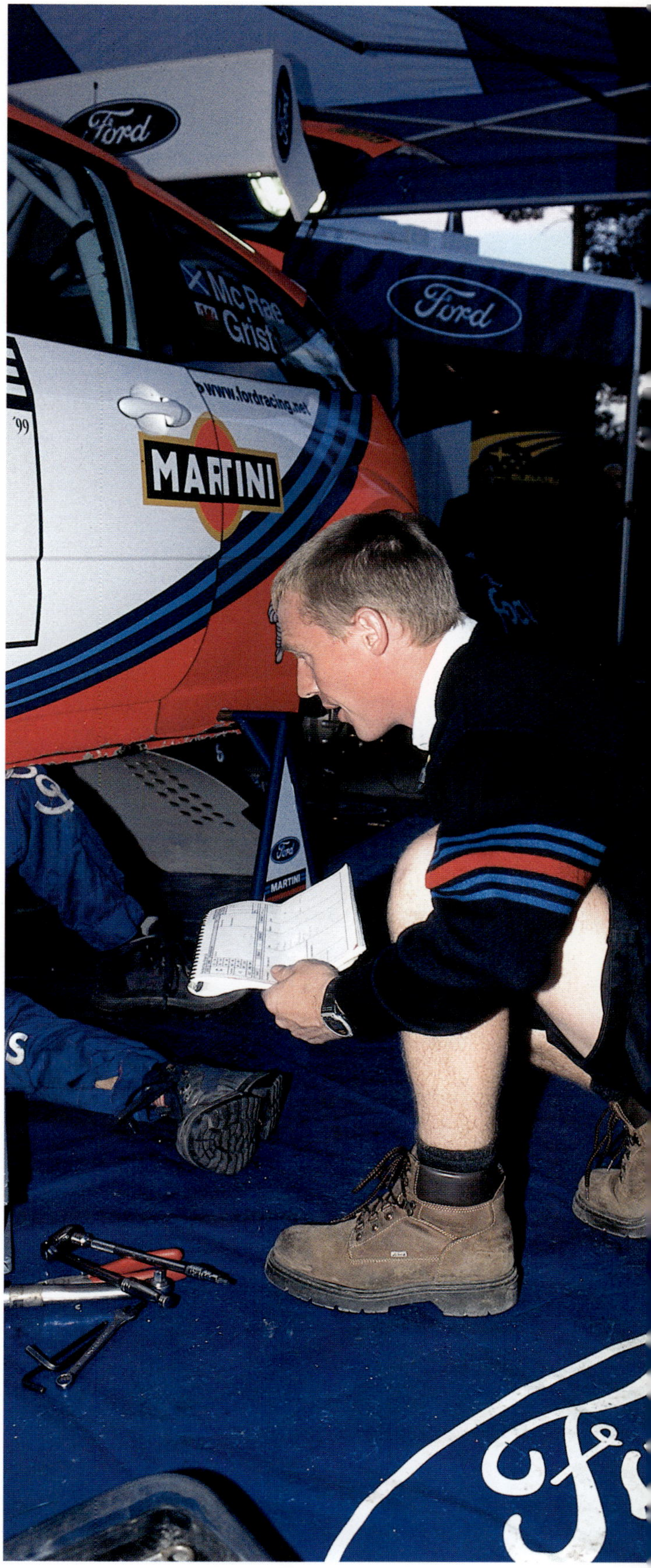

Martin Wilkinson … always in control.

Dr Ravin Naik, Team Doctor

The fitness of the drivers, and the rest of the team, assumes ever greater importance in rallying. All sports have made enormous strides in scientific health care and the Ford World Rally Championship team brought in Dr Naik to take their pulse at the beginning of 1998. He has a sports medicine clinic at Sheffield Wednesday Football Club and his other clients include Sheffield Eagles rugby league club and the world champion boxer Naseem Hamed. The former Wimbledon FC manager, Joe Kinnear, was grateful for Dr Naik's expertise and facilities when he had a heart attack before a match at Hillsborough. Dr Naik and his colleagues saved Kinnear's life.

'It was the day we got back from Kenya,' Dr Naik recalled. 'I was in the dressing room area and the Wimbledon physio came in to see me. He said Joe wasn't feeling too well. Unfortunately their club doctor wasn't there so I had a look at him. He wasn't looking too good but I was in the fortunate position of having all the equipment in the clinic and being able to give him the necessary treatment. The other very fortunate thing was that the paramedics were on hand and able to take him straight up to hospital.'

Dr Naik was drawn to Ford by a small ad in the *British Medical Journal*. He read that an international motorsport team required a doctor.

'Obviously the priority here is to look after all the drivers and co-drivers, and to make sure they are in peak physical and psychological condition to compete. There's little point in Ford spending multimillion pounds developing a new car if the people who are piloting the car are not up to their own optimum level of performance. The other thing I do, which to me is equally important, is look after all the team, the mechanics, the engineers, PR staff, media guests, etc., which basically covers all aspects of primary care and medicine, so it's quite busy.'

He works on the rallies in tandem with the team's physio-trainer, Alan Muckle.

'Alan and I travel around together during an event and before the event. Fortunately, we're both fairly keen on our own fitness and do a certain amount of training together, so training is second nature to both of us. The important thing is that we both have higher training in that field, so we are able to adapt elements of coaching to fit with the drivers' requirements. Apart from the stamina

Engineers and mechanics work against the clock.

training, there are also things we do with regard to hand–eye co-ordination and foot speed, which are more specific to the sport.

'We pay particular attention to making sure the drivers drink the correct amount of fluid, and the right composition. There's no point in drinking coffee or Coke. It has to be drinks which contain the correct amounts of salts and carbohydrates.

'Diet is another factor which we pay particular attention to. We work with the people at the motorhome, guide them on the correct types of food. At the start of the year we get a full breakdown of what the drivers normally eat, and set out the requirements in accordance with fairly strict guidelines which sports dieticians follow. You aim for 65 per cent carbohydrates, 15 per cent protein and 20 per cent fat in the total composition of the diet. It's actually a lot more carbohydrate than people realise. A driver like Colin will be using about 4,000 calories a day on an event.'

But then Colin has also been known to enjoy his burgers and a few other things that might not figure too prominently on Dr Naik's diet sheet.

'Allegedly,' the doctor responded earnestly. 'Fortunately he started this regime of fitness at Subaru. That's the main reason we brought Alan over. It was good for Colin to have someone he'd worked with and trusted, someone he understood. There's little point in being the best, most qualified scientist in the world if the person you're trying to deal with hasn't got a clue what you're talking about and can't relate to it. Alan already had a working relationship with Colin.

He's rare in being able to go through a bad patch, then forget it

'Now he is very switched on and aware that if he wants to go on competing for the next few years then he'll have to pay attention to these elements. At the moment he is as fit as any sports person I've worked with. That includes professional rugby players, professional soccer players. In a very different way, but in terms of his cardiovascular performance he is right up there.

'The other very important thing in most sports is the psychological approach. Colin's very strong from that point of view in that he's one of those rare sports people who's able to go through a bad patch, as all sportsmen do, but then completely forget about it. So he may do a stage where something's gone wrong through no fault of his own, and he's able to ignore that and focus completely on the next one. Whether you are in motorsport, football, rugby or any other sport, that is a very important asset.'

The physical and psychological checks begin first thing in the morning during rallies.

'Alan wakes up the drivers and we have breakfast with them. We take them to the start, where we chat about things, make sure they're switched on and ready for the day ahead, make sure they haven't got any problems or underlying worries. If there is a niggle, Alan is there to give them a massage. We make sure when they're having breakfast they are having the right foods at the start of the day. We make sure all the drivers have a certain amount of fluid before they even get in the car, half a litre to a litre. If you started competing in a dehydrated state things would rapidly get worse. It's not untypical for drivers to be losing between nine and ten litres of fluid in a 12-hour competitive period. And it is estimated one per cent dehydration leads to a ten per cent decrease in physical and psychological performance.

'We drop them off at the start and make sure the car starts. Although what we as doctors and athletic trainers can do about that I don't know! But we inform HQ. And then we follow the drivers to the first service park. We trail them in a doctor's car. During the services we make sure there is fluid in the car and make sure the drivers are wearing dry clothing. It's just a case of making sure they are comfortable.

'It's absolutely vital they are eating when they come in, at times when they don't want to eat and drink, and really we have to almost force it upon them. But they're in a routine now where they know it's necessary for them to be performing.

'They can be up at five in the morning and still competing at eight in the evening, and I can't think of many sports where that would be the case. It's not unhealthy or dangerous. It's just the nature of the sport. It's important that in the planning for the year you make sure the drivers are able to sustain the workrate. It's not just the physical element, it's the psychological element also. It's difficult to get the time with them when they come in for the short services because they need to talk to the team boss, the engineers, and they need to eat something. But we're always there if they have got any problems.

'At the end of the day we pick the drivers up from parc fermé, take them back to the hotel, and Alan will work on them for half to three quarters of an hour, just give them a massage and things like that. Obviously if they need any treatment we have a certain amount of equipment which we carry around with us. The most common thing with drivers at the end of the day is fatigue, which is natural. The physical problems they can suffer from are really back related: neck, upper back, lower back. And then the odd tweaks and twinges that most sports people get. In the case of a driver, normally the right arm, feet, calves. But again, if they have a correct programme of exercise before they get in the car, then those problems are far fewer than they would normally have been.'

Alan Muckle, Physio-trainer

McRae and Grist were not the only signings from Subaru. Muckle moved over also to keep the pair in shape and on physical course. An ex-marine, he has clinics in Bristol and Newport, but for much of the year works for Ford, dovetailing with Dr Naik.

'My main aim is to look after the drivers, medically, with physiotherapy and sports massage, and my second role is to be their fitness trainer,' he said. 'So on every event I come along to all the recces and take the training with the drivers. We do lots of work on mountain bikes. It's really the endurance side of it. We can go out for maybe three hours at a time. The drivers enjoy cycling. You can have all sorts of ways of working on fitness but if they don't enjoy it then it's no good. So it's getting them into the habit of mountain biking, which they can also do at home.

'And the other thing is that it gets them away from rallying completely. They get off into the mountains and just chill out. But believe me, they do work hard at it. We all push each other. We go to fantastic places and enjoy the scenery, so it's a psychological thing as well. You don't have to drag them to do anything. They're all

Alan Muckle (left) and Dr Ravin Naik ensure the team are fit to perform.

pretty clued up on what they have to do. It's as important for the co-driver as it is for the driver.

'Colin is in good nick. He's not spent as much time training this year as he would have liked because of the development of the car. That's taken up a lot of his time. But we've settled into a nice routine. Away from rallies as well. I'll go to his house in Scotland and take him for some sessions there, and we have a training programme for when there are longer gaps between the rallies.

They are long, long days in rallying and the drivers need stamina

'It's important to give them information about what we're doing. It's no good telling them "do that." They have to understand what's happening when they're doing it. And the more knowledge you can give them the more likely they are to stick to it and understand what's going on.

'I think there's still a lot to be done in this field, especially in motorsport, but probably in most sports. I worked with the England Rugby Union as a professional coach, and fitness levels in the last eight to ten years have gone up dramatically. My background is the military. I did 16 years in the Marines and without the fitness you couldn't do what you were asked to do. They are long, long days in rallying, and they need that stamina.

'The new lads coming into it will probably be educated that little bit more and understand what it can do for them. You only have to look around a service park to see the physique of drivers. Maybe not some of those at the top, who have been around for a while, but the younger ones are pretty lean. Ten years ago you would probably have seen a totally different attitude from drivers in terms of fitness and training, and diet. So there is a better understanding of what goes on behind the wheel. You don't just sit in the car and drive any more. You need to be sharper than that.

'We do a mainly carbohydrate diet – a lot of pasta and rice – and vegetables and salad. The water intake is very important. We use a solution which gets absorbed into the system much quicker and has a nice taste to it. It's blackcurrant and apple, quite commonly used. The drivers prefer that. In hot countries they'll drink up to eight litres during the day. When they open the car doors the heat just whooshes at you. In the evenings they'll keep drinking to top up the levels for the next morning.

'They'll probably have cereal for breakfast, at the hotel. Then they may have some more cereal or toast when they get to the service park after a long drive. Perhaps some fruit salad. At midday they'll have pasta or rice. At the end of the day I'll give them a massage.

'Two things here. One, it will relax them and enable them to sleep better because they'll be in a better state of mind; two, it's a special massage and as I'm going around the body I'm looking for potential problems, which you can have without knowing. It's preventative. What's really important is the back and the neck after all that jarring around with the helmet on. We probably need to do more on the neck muscles, especially for the co-driver, sitting in that position, head down in the notes all the time. It's not so bad for the driver because his shoulders are up and he's getting a little more support for the neck. Regardless of the sport you play, fatigue is always the limiting factor and the earlier you fatigue the more mistakes you will make. So for the co-driver it is just as important.

'I've been working with Colin for two years now and I see the improvement in him. He's got a gym at his place so he works there as well as on the mountain bike. Maybe if we'd got hold of him at 25 instead of 28 we could have made a bigger difference, but he's no problem now. He's got natural ability but as other things start catching up with him and he gets older, it becomes even more important for him to work at this side of things to stay in that No. 1 spot.'

Father, right-hand man and ever patriotic Scotsman.

Jimmy McRae, Gravel Car

The drivers and co-drivers make their reconnaissance trips through the rally stages several days before the event proper and by the time they return in competition there may be significant changes to the condition of the roads. It is the job of the gravel crews to identify those changes on runs just ahead of the rally cars. The gravel car driver should be perceptive and knowledgeable – as well as handy at the wheel – and Colin McRae has the utmost faith in the man paving his way. That man is his father Jimmy, five times British Rally Champion.

'We're checking Colin's and Nicky's notes from when they did the recce, which could have been seven or eight days earlier,' Jimmy said. 'The weather could have changed, the road surface could have changed. In the forests there could have been logging, with trucks going in and out, so the roads could be rutted. They might have had a machine in to touch up and repair the roads. These are all the things we've got to look for and if there's the slightest difference to the notes we've got to spot it.

I used to be a wee bit worried but you can always temper a thoroughbred

'I'm very much involved in tyre choice as well. We know what tyres can do in certain conditions and try to work out the best choice over the two or three stages coming up. A particular tyre may be better on one but not so good on another, so you have to compromise to come up with the best tyre choice. I'll often sit down with Colin at the end of the day and discuss how things have gone, or join the team debriefings. Sometimes I put my bit in and get involved in that.'

And much more besides. Like management.

'I look after Colin's affairs, and Alister's [his other rallying son], and I still do bits and pieces with other people as well. When Colin got the offer from Ford it was very much something we talked over together. I was very much involved in the discussions and meetings and basically did the deal. It was a very difficult decision for us. He'd been so long with Subaru but you have to look forward. This car is definitely the next generation of cars. It's aerodynamically better and the weight distribution is better, although it's not completely right at the moment. It's improving all the time.'

So, he believes in his son and he had little doubt that Colin would reach this level.

'When Colin puts his mind to something he wants to do he'll do it. I knew from an early age, when he started rallying, that he definitely had the speed and the ability. He just had to temper it and hone it down a wee bit. I never really gave him lessons. He sat beside me in testing and that sort of thing. I co-drove for him in one rally, a national event. In this game you're learning all the time. You learn something new and still look back and say, "I shouldn't have done that." Rallying is very much down to mileage. The more miles you do in the car, the better you become. If there is a problem, experience can sometimes help in rectifying it.

'I worried a bit about Colin when he was younger, but not now. It's a relatively safe sport. The cars are very strong. There's a big, big safety factor built into these things. Accidents can happen, but accidents can happen in the home as well. I used to be concerned a wee bit when he was criticised about his driving. But you can always temper a thoroughbred and trim off the rough edges. It's very difficult with somebody who can drive at 85 or even 90 per cent to get that extra 10 per cent. It's sometimes impossible. But if you've got somebody who can drive 105 or 110 per cent, you can hone that back down. I think one of Colin's good points is that when the chips are really down he can just come up with that extra ten per cent.

'Occasionally I go out on the stage to watch him, where we get time, maybe at the end of a leg when we've finished. It's not just to see what Colin's doing but also to see what the other cars are doing.

Sometimes you can learn a wee bit from that. Maybe the car is not as good in certain conditions as another car. It does give me a buzz to see Colin driving, especially when he's winning.'

Rallying has long been a family affair for the McRaes. Margaret McRae has been a fervent supporter out in the forests, following the fortunes of Jimmy, Colin and Alister. Their other son, Stuart, would lend a hand with the catering and opted for that route in life.

'Margaret still comes out to the rallies occasionally but not so much since Hollie was born,' Jimmy said. 'She prefers to look after Hollie and let Alison get out with Colin. It's been hard for Alister following Colin but he's doing pretty well and hopefully he can keep progressing. It was going to be a lot worse still for Stuart, too much of a gamble, so he never really got interested in competing. He has his own business now, café and sandwich bar and a bit of catering. He's happy with what he's doing and he's found his niche in life.'

The rallying landscape has undergone major changes since Jimmy was competing at his peak and his sons were wee boys.

'Events were much longer then, four and five days, into the night and through the night. I call it office hours now,' he said chuckling. 'It was probably tougher but at least in those days you could back off slightly on the rougher stages, and pick your way through. Now, with the shorter format of the rallies, you can't afford to back off. You've got to try and drive these things flat out. The days when you could have a puncture and still not lose a place are definitely gone. If you have a puncture now you drop out of the top ten and that's it. In those days it was a different discipline.

'Nowadays I think rallying is going the correct way to get it to the media. It's difficult to do that when a rally is over five days and into the night. If this is the way to get it on TV then it's got to be done.

'Training is obviously a big part of it now, but I did try to keep fit when I was doing the British Championship and some of the World Championship rounds. I did cycling and running, though maybe not to the extent they do now. I tried to be sensible with my eating and that definitely helped. If you're feeling a bit unfit and not eating the right things your mind loses that sharpness.

'I really enjoy what I'm doing now. A lot of people say it's glamorous but it's hard work when you're doing 14 rounds. And it's pretty unsocial hours gravel noting. We start two or three hours earlier than the drivers. But on the plus side I get a lot of pleasure and satisfaction out of it.

Breakfast up! Stu and Di Spires at the ready with traditional fried eggs and bacon.

You know you're doing an important job, you've still got an involvement and you're playing your part in the team effort.'

Di Spires, Motorhome

Just as an army marches on its stomach, so a motorsport crew needs its fill to take on the opposition. Di and Stuart Spires have been feeding and watering teams for more than 20 years. In Formula One circles they are an institution. They decided against having a family to pursue their culinary careers on the road and adopted squads of mechanics and drivers. They are known in the Grand Prix paddock as Mum and Dad. Their list of drivers includes Nigel Mansell and Michael Schumacher. To their 'family' they have provided not only sustenance but also a friendly chat and sometimes a shoulder to cry on.

They work with Ford in Formula One and, along with their regular colleagues, Graham and Tracey Ogden, have taken on the World Rally Championship also. On the rallies they are joined by M-Sport's Pamela Brise. Their Ford blue bus criss-crosses Europe on a perpetual mission, taking in test sessions as well as races and rallies. It bears the names of the Stewart Grand Prix drivers, Rubens Barrichello and Johnny Herbert, as well as the Ford Martini drivers and co-drivers. At the race circuit they cook in a canvas kitchen, on a rally they have a van, and in both perform minor gastronomic miracles.

Di said: 'I think the boys in rallying are more appreciative than Formula One people, who have come to expect getting well looked after. These boys are grateful for anything you do for them. And they'll do anything to help us because they understand our problems, being constantly on the move. They really are fantastic people here. Formula One boys arrive for a race in their designer suits, carrying their briefcases. These lads turn up in their overalls carrying their toolboxes. They work really hard and in all sorts of weather, and get paid nothing like as much as the Formula One mechanics.

'They work really hard and in all sorts of weather.'

FORD MARTINI RALLY TEAM
Acropolis Rally – 6-9 June 1999

Identity	*Vehicle*	*Personnel*	
7 'Nicky'	Ford Focus WRC S10 FMC	Colin McRae	Nicky Grist
8 'Fred'	Ford Focus WRC S8 FMC	Thomas Rådström	Fred Gallagher
Super 1 SP1	Galaxy S412 WVW	M. Wilson C. Goodman G. Steiner	J. Millington N. Arnfield
Super 2 SP2	Transit Van	G. Black	M. Ineson
Super 3 SP3	Galaxy S453 XTW	F. Rowlands G. Seesing	D. Revens H. Robson
Mech 1 M1	Galaxy S454 XTW	M. Wilkinson T. Gahan M. MacDonald	D. Bell G. Clayton
Mech 2 M2	Transit Minibus T541 JVW	N. Smith R. Warmisham P. Bradshaw	R. Barton D. Mason
Van 2 S2	Iveco S2 FMC	S. Armstrong	S. Garner
Van 3 S3	Iveco S3 FMC	K. Watson	R. Saunders
Van 4 S4	Iveco S4 FMC	I. Dodd	M. Tennant
Doctor	Galaxy	R. Naik	A. Muckle
Motorhome 1 (F1)	P3 FMC & Truck T414 KAB	S. & D. Spires P. Brise	G. & T. Ogden
Gravel 1	Escort Cosworth N870 GNO	J. McRae	C. Roy
Gravel 2	Escort Cosworth N929 FHK	G. Barth	J. Skallman
Gravel Service	Iveco K485 TKP	W. Crozier	
Gravel Runner	Escort Cosworth N507 GVW	A. Wright	
PR	Loan car	P. Baker	M. Whitaker
Press	Loan car	D. Gallagher	
Press	Media Centre	M. Wilford	

'Mind you, they prefer to be busy and moving around. At San Remo we were in one place and the boys were just hanging around for two or three days. They're not used to that and all they could do, because they were so bored, was eat. They said they couldn't stand that every rally because they'd be 20 stones at the end of the season. They'd much rather be rolling around in the mud and being up in the mountains. That's why they're in rallying.

'The drivers have to eat certain things and they're pretty good about that, but they do like their treats now and then. Colin and Nicky will have their fruit salad as they're supposed to do but then might sneak into the kitchen for a bacon sandwich. Colin likes a bar of chocolate, as well. I put some in the fridge for him. He knows where I hide them, behind the bottles. It was the same with Michael Schumacher. And they love their cups of tea.

Sometimes we move three times a day – as the cars go we're packing away

'They tend to be more relaxed and chatty than Formula One drivers. Not quite so intense. But they're intense when they need to be. They seem to be able to switch, whereas today's Formula One drivers are finding it a big problem to switch. They don't seem to be able to enjoy themselves. Colin will have a chat when he comes to the motorhome. He'll say he's doing OK or got a problem or whatever, but he's quite shy really. He always gets out of the car and comes to the boys. He's not one for playing the superstar. Nicky's fantastic, a lovely man. And Fred Gallagher and the other drivers. They're all nice people. I've not seen any tantrums in rallying yet – but I've seen a few in Formula One.

'We said we'd try to do both Formula One and rallying in 1999 and see how it went. We're doing nine rallies this year, the European ones. It's a bit punishing because we can be away from our home in England for three months at a time. After the Hungarian Grand Prix we have to go straight to the rally in Finland. We set off on the Sunday evening and get to the Austrian border at three o'clock on Monday morning. From there we drive through Germany and Denmark to Sweden and get the ferry to Finland. After the rally we're straight back down to the Belgian Grand Prix. We bring in someone to share the driving with Stuart for that trip.

'But at least that gives some variety. When we were at the Benetton Grand Prix team it was race-test-race-test and ultimately that just gets to you. Now we have a change of scenery and people. Rallying is totally different from Formula One. Each has its appeal.

'You don't have time to be formal in rallying. We move three times a day on some rallies, so as soon as the cars are gone we're taking things down and packing away. The days are longer than in Formula One but you can at least sit down and relax a bit. In Formula One you're there 18 hours and you're on your feet all the time. You can't hang around and have a chat. You have some early starts in rallying. In Portugal we had three 3 o'clock mornings, and we hadn't been in bed till midnight. I think we had 17 hours sleep over the five days there. When you get five hours in one night it's quite a luxury.

'What I'm still getting used to is not really knowing what's going on in the rally. In Formula One we have the TV screens so we can see who's doing what in practice and the race. Here you have to find someone who knows what's happening. I can't work out who's leading overall. There are people here who can analyse the different stages and work it out. The tyres alone are a science. I find it amazing to hear them talking about the different types, cuts and studs and so on. Formula One is really easy by comparison. And it's all such a fantastic logistical exercise. I'm only just getting used to their maps, these "tulips" [directions in the route book, which have the appearance of the flower] as they call them. We have to find our own way like the rest of them. You do feel as though you're involved.'

chapter eight

Reluctant superstar

Picture all the images conjured by the word 'superstar' and the chances are Colin McRae will fit none of them. It is perhaps the biggest compliment he can be paid. He makes no pretence at being sophisticated, nor does he feel the compulsion to be gratuitously yobbish; he neither courts attention nor attracts it by aping Greta Garbo. Although he is worth millions and has bases in some of Europe's most desired locations, he is most content back home in Scotland among his kinsfolk. That, too, might be considered an affectation in some, but those who know McRae are adamant it is not. The more you hear of how much he has changed, the more you suspect he hasn't. He could have merged into the anonymous mass as a factory worker or a farmhand and been essentially the same Colin McRae.

McRae in party mode, with wife Alison.

He would doubtless be more at ease in such workplaces than he is enduring some of the ancillary duties associated with superstardom. He remains, at times, transparently uncomfortable, if not clumsy, on public display. Stuffy functions and polite tittle tattle with people he has never met, much less wishes to meet again, appeal to him about as much as a sticking throttle. He would probably run a mile to avoid the next media interview. He has never been considered by journalists as one of the best 'talks' and yet some of his unscripted remarks, fresh from the soul, have produced sizzling copy. Candid, unprogrammed, uncomplicated, McRae is what you see and what you tend to get. Driving rally cars is what comes naturally. The rest he could do without.

Beneath the quiet exterior lurks a strong will that can be rebellious

'I'd rather just get on with what I do, away from all the attention,' he says in that monotone voice which again makes no concession to stage management. 'But it's becoming more and more difficult to do that. There's more attention all the time. Going home is the best way I can deal with it. It's nice to get down to our place in Spain when I can and we've got our place in Monaco as well, but I enjoy going back to Scotland more than anything. We can't spend too much time there and that makes it that much nicer when we can get there.

'All the family is there. Alison's as well as mine. I can switch off there, just by going home and having something like a normal family life. It's more important than ever now we've got Hollie. Fortunately she's good and I still get my sleep. She's probably spoiled us for having another. I can appreciate the simple things even more. I cut the grass and find it enjoyable. Honestly! Just doing the things everybody else does. These are the things I miss.

'I can see old friends again, go out for dinner with them. The good thing about going back home is that although everybody obviously follows what Alister and I are doing, we can go down to the local pub for a drink and join in with the chat as though we're in there every Friday night, and nobody mentions motorsport. If they were all talking about the rallying we wouldn't go because we wouldn't enjoy it. But we know we can go there and just relax.'

You sense it suits him to perpetuate the impression he is the shy, retiring type, content to nestle in the bosom of his clan. And yet beneath the quiet, reticent exterior lurks a strong will that occasionally surfaces in a show of defiance, anger and even rebellion. When he was with Subaru he bucked at team orders to hold station behind his team-mate, Carlos Sainz, in Catalunya and so hand the Championship advantage to the local man. Victory on the RAC, and with it the 1995 title, put the record straight. He experienced his most costly confrontation with authority after bowling over three people in his anxiety to get away from a service point in Argentina. None was hurt but the FIA felt he had to be taught a lesson and fined him 75,000 dollars. As if to rub salt in the wound, the hearing was fixed during the recce for the 1000 Lakes Rally, so denying him crucial preparation time on the event that requires the most preparation. His career has also been punctuated by blunt pronouncements of dissatisfaction, while he in turn has taken more than his share of criticism.

'There is a bit more to me than the shy, quiet type,' he says with a self-satisfied grin. 'Now and again, anyway. The frustrations can build up inside you and it depends on what kind of person you are whether you let them out when they're just simmering or wait till they're boiling. I tend to wait until it gets to the point where I'm too upset to keep it in any longer.'

His outburst over the water pump issue being a case in point?

'Yes, but I think speaking out like that can also be a good thing. That was one of

McRae is not always so cool.

those situations where I spoke out because I was obviously very angry and I said things that weren't true. I blamed Ford and the engineers for not getting it right and when you look at the situation, they were all under pressure and they did a tremendous job. So that was wrong and it's something I regret having said. But there again it didn't do an awful lot of harm because at least they then knew something about me and how I felt, that I was committed and really cared and wanted to get it right and deliver results.'

McRae's first months with Ford served as a cameo of his career with Subaru: the sublime, breathtaking driving, the successes and the ructions. David Richards, the Subaru team principal, tried the stick and carrot approach with him, publicly admonishing him, dropping him from events, even hinting at the sack, then building him up with a paean and an embrace. McRae is grateful for the opportunity Subaru gave him, but the stinging words have left their scars.

Richard Burns, British rival.

'The '94 season was probably my lowest ebb,' he reflects solemnly. 'There was a lot more to that than meets the eye. It wasn't just the mistakes I made and I know I did make mistakes that year. The team were having a lot of problems as well. David said a few things in the Press that maybe he regretted saying afterwards. In the heat of the moment you say things that you regret. I know that as well as anyone.

'But the fact was that he always had confidence in me and he kept me there so I think that speaks for itself. The important thing was that he knew, and I knew, that it was going to work, and it was just a matter of working it out, bringing the spark back. I wouldn't say 1995 was a comeback. I was never coming back from anywhere. I was always coming from the bottom up. It was a bit rocky for a wee while, and then it smoothed out again.

'I think these experiences made me better. I've learned from my mistakes and I think you always are learning. You can never afford to believe you have learned everything there is to learn.'

McRae learned to drive in a family environment where it was second nature. It is now such an instinctive process he finds explaining his talent for car control an impossible task.

'I really don't think about it an awful lot,' he says. 'A lot of drivers can tell you how they do it but I don't think I can. I'd never be an instructor because I couldn't really tell anybody how to drive. If they asked me a question I'd have to think, "How do I do that?" It's just an automatic thing.'

McRae's further education in rallying brought him into contact with ditches and worse, yet he has no regrets about his style or his course. His philosophy was based on the ultimate advantage of pure pace. The subtleties could be acquired with the passing years, but speed was the indispensable raw material.

'It really depends on your approach. You can take a different approach and start slowly. I think it takes you longer to do that. If you start out going quickly you learn faster. You're trying to achieve a certain level and if you actually go beyond that level and crash a few times, it's easier to come back to that level than if you're building up slowly all the time. I think Richard Burns is an example of a driver who was very steady to start with, then got quicker and quicker. But it's taken him quite a long time to reach this level.

'The other thing is that as a young driver you need to be noticed. If you win one rally and crash on two you will get noticed. Somebody will be watching you. If you finish fifth or sixth on three rallies people will tend not to look at you so much.'

It is unnerving merely to hear him talk blithely of this crash course. He has had a few spectacular offs, notably a 30-metre plunge from a road during testing in Portugal, an accident which indicated the direction of his career in the early part of 1994. He admitted he feared for his life in that moment, a rare submission to what the outside world would consider normal emotions. He has, however, been fortunate in avoiding serious injury and potentially permanent damage to his self-belief.

'I never really think about hurting myself,' he says perhaps not wanting to think about it now. 'You don't have time to have fear when you're on the stage. You wouldn't be able to do this if you started thinking about the dangers too much. I've had a few accidents over the years, of course, but nothing bad. This year's Acropolis could have been the worst. We were definitely lucky there. But I've never been badly hurt. You can have a pretty simple accident and break a wrist or something if it gets caught in the wheel. You could say that was a bad one because you injured yourself. But you can completely destroy a car and walk away from it. The good thing is that these cars are very strong and very safe.

'Spectators can be a real danger on certain rallies. We've had problems in the past at places like Portugal and Spain with people getting too close to the road or even on it. That's something else you can't allow yourself to think too much about. Photographers are the biggest problem. They want the best picture so I can understand that. Just like us, they are very competitive. I did clip someone once, on the inside of a bend, but luckily without causing serious injury. When you're on the Safari spectators aren't a problem out in the bush but the animals can be a distraction, more than anything. You have to be very wary.

'I think in rallying what you have to do above all is believe in yourself. I've always believed I can find that little bit extra when I need it, that it's always there. I have believed I would be the best since the beginning. You've got to believe there's no reason why the other guy should be able to drive any quicker than you. Even when you start, you've got to believe you can drive quicker – maybe not as well because he's got experience – but quicker every now and then, even on just one stage. If you can do it once you know it's only a matter of

A broken thumb is a minor discomfort McRae can cope with as he proved in Kenya.

Encroaching spectators are an occupational hazard.

time before you can do it regularly.'

McRae has been winning stages regularly for years but contends he has not yet reached his optimum level of performance as a rally driver.

'I think that only comes when you have the right balance of speed and experience. There comes a point where you don't get any quicker, but it's the experience that makes you the complete driver. The other important thing is the motivation, and I still have that. I'm not saying I can get much better but I can still fine tune things, just the bits and pieces, to make me a more complete driver.

'You look at a driver like Carlos, who's never been the quickest around, but he's always been very consistent, and every now and then he can push very quickly. People were saying a couple of years ago that Juha was going downhill but he won in Argentina and Finland, which shows you can never be sure. People are bound to have bad rallies or bad years. You can't keep going at 100 per cent all the time.'

Since McRae is frequently likened to Senna and Schumacher, it would serve as an intriguing insight to compare their

thoughts on the pursuit of driving perfection. Senna said he felt the greatest challenge was within himself. Schumacher says he has never driven the car that has found his limits. Alas, McRae argues there can be no realistic comparison.

'Rallying is different from racing in that the first time we drive a stage in competition is the first time we drive it at full speed. We have to go by our pace notes and have absolute confidence in them, trust the co-driver and have the confidence to take a sixth gear corner flat, as you need to. On a race track it's a different situation. You know the circuit, you practise on it at full speed, so you're able to say when you've done your absolute best lap, that you couldn't have gone any quicker. It's possible to analyse what you're doing far more easily.

'For us there are a lot of places in a rally where you brake too much or you go just a bit too quickly and go a bit wider than you want to be. When you consider all the circumstances, it's pretty good that we can drive with anything like the precision we do the first time we drive through a stage at speed.'

Confidence and trust are words that figure prominently in McRae's vocabulary. They are the pillars of his relationship with the coterie of people he has had about him: from his father to his co-driver.

'It's good having my dad around because, of course, I trust him. He helps out a lot on the management stuff, running the office, dealing with the bank accounts and all the bits and pieces. And then with the other job he does, the gravel notes, you need to have 100 per cent confidence in the person who's doing that. The same applies to the co-driver. If he gets his side of it wrong then it normally results in me getting it wrong.'

The chemistry between driver and co-driver should also be right. McRae parted company with his long-time navigator Derek Ringer at the end of 1996 in what were generally considered unsavoury circumstances. For all the expressions of public gratitude he received, Ringer made no bones about the fact he was sacked and McRae is frank enough to say he prefers working with Nicky Grist.

During the recce you can have a bit of fun in the car, a bit of a joke

'All these guys at this level are very much the same,' McRae expands. 'It's like the drivers. We're all very much the same. I think the important thing is the character of the person, and how you get on with the guy, because you spend most of your life stuck in the car with him. The relationship I've got with Nicky is a lot better than it was with Derek. It's more enjoyable. During the recce you can have a bit of fun in the car, a bit of a joke. It's not too serious all the time. We're serious when we have to be and on the professional side of the job I've got total trust in Nicky. I always prefer to have him with me in testing. We do the job together. He's well organised and on top of it all the time. He knows he has to be. He can't afford to get it wrong.'

The McRae–Grist partnership ran for two years at Subaru before a combination of circumstances – the passage of time and the right opportunity – convinced the Scotsman he had to move on.

'Coming to Ford was the right move at the right time for me. Things might have gone better at Subaru in the last couple of years but we had a lot of little mechanical problems. I think it's fair to say we lost one Championship, if not two, because of that. It wasn't bad, but it could have been better. And it was becoming the same old thing every year. I think you really have to change things before it gets too stale. I think at Subaru it was beginning to get a bit stale.

'Ford's whole attitude and commitment to rallying, and motorsport in general, had changed dramatically. Certainly Ford in rallying over the previous few years almost looked half-hearted to me. They really started to come round when Malcolm took over. Once I saw the difference Malcolm was making to the operation, and saw the way Ford Motor Company were getting behind it, I knew I had to make the move.'

He knew also there would be difficulties to negotiate in the early stages of the Focus's development. He was as startled as anyone by his performance on the Monte Carlo.

'I was very surprised we started so well because it wasn't until the day before Monte Carlo, when we were doing the shakedown, that we started to make some real progress with the car. We were really struggling up to that point. Through all the testing we did we had the wrong weather conditions, problems with the car, just so many things going against us. We really had our backs to the wall. So Monte Carlo was a very pleasant surprise once we actually got going. All of a sudden we found the car was competitive.'

So much for all that pre-season propaganda about 'the testing going so well'. Part of the mind game, of course. Less surprising to McRae was the emergence of Tommi Mäkinen as the pace-setter in yet another Championship. Victory in New Zealand – where McRae had overtaken him only to be sabotaged by a mysterious misfire – gave the Finn a clear vision of his fourth consecutive title.

'I always thought of Tommi as my

biggest threat because of his record. The sport really could do with someone different winning the Championship but all credit to Tommi. And don't get me wrong, he's a tremendous driver and a friend of mine. You know for sure there are certain drivers you can come up against on the last day of a rally and feel fairly confident you can beat them. Richard, for instance. If I was 15 seconds behind Richard on the last day I'd feel I could beat him. With Tommi on the other hand I wouldn't be so confident. I would still have a go, but I wouldn't have the same feeling I could do it.'

Just about the ultimate challenge in rallying is to beat Mäkinen in Finland. It is perhaps even more daunting a task than to outpace McRae in his home rally. McRae yearns to add the rally still known to many as the 1000 Lakes to his c.v.

'The one I'd really like to win is the 1000 Lakes because it's such a specialist event and you need the experience there more than anywhere else,' he said, before embarking on the 1999 event. 'What makes it so difficult is that you have crests and then blind corners. You've got to get it right but still keep up the speed.'

McRae and Mäkinen are renowned for driving fastest, and leaping highest and longest. However, winning rallies in every corner of the world and putting together successful Championship campaigns demands versatility and intelligence as well as raw pace and brute determination. Wilson rates McRae's 1999 win in Portugal as his finest because of its judgement and control from the front. McRae, true to type, stands by his maiden World Championship victory, in New Zealand, in 1993, when he stymied the assault of François Delecour on one of the great high-speed events.

'That still has to be my best. New Zealand has always been one of my favourite rallies. The stages are very fast and flowing, and challenging to drive. To be honest, nowadays the standards of all the rallies are pretty good so there aren't any I really dislike. Some rallies still suffer

The author puts on a brave face but McRae looks less than confident in his new co-driver.

from a poor level of spectator safety, which does make it difficult, but from a driver's point of view you see each rally as a challenge and your aim is always to be the quickest. You can always learn that bit more wherever you are. You take note of who's doing what and just keep an eye on things. Any little thing you pick up can help you on that particular rally.'

All this talk fuels the inevitable curiosity: Just what IS it like to be in the rally car with Colin McRae? It is time to find out.

This was not the 1000 Lakes, New Zealand or the RAC, but the test stage in Cumbria still seemed authentic and awesome enough. Lowther Forest is 16 miles south of Cockermouth. The start of the 2.73-mile stage is just off the public road at the point where it crests the exposed, wild moor. Any unsuspecting tourist passing through and encountering this collection of service and hospitality vehicles, and Malcolm Wilson's helicopter, in the bleak wilderness must have wondered if the aliens had finally made it. The sheep, patently accustomed to the antics of these rallying folk with their growling machines, grazed regardless.

The novices took off their helmets to reveal glaring eyes the size of golf balls

McRae would be driving Thomas Rådström's Acropolis car. It was the fourth Focus World Rally Car built, and was fitted with new engine and tyres for this exercise. Nobody mentioned a new sump. A bit disconcerting, that. More comforting was the back-up: eight technicians, two engineers, ten marshals, a stage controller, a doctor, the helicopter, a service truck, the Ford bus, one catering truck, three chefs and a Focus WRC showcar. Even a showcar!

The skies over the distant peaks were as savage and forbidding as any of the night stages on RACs of yesteryear. And this was mid-June. The ubiquitous Stuart Spires battened down the hatches and mischievously speculated on the effects of rain – to the stage and McRae's sense of humour. If it was meant to be unnerving it worked. The queue of journalists guesting as McRae's co-drivers on this media day giggled hideously, thankful for some kind of release. Waiting to make a bungee-jump or a parachute jump must be like this.

McRae stepped from the bus in his working gear and stood by his car, chatting to the mechanics. He is taller than you imagine today's drivers to be, narrow in the hip, wide in the shoulder, although that may be exaggerated by the line of his suit. He glanced, in mild amusement, at his first victim, who was trying to put on a helmet. A team member offered unhelpful advice: 'Just hold your breath for about two minutes 50 seconds.'

The first co-driver strapped in, McRae crunched the car into reverse with the kind of racket you dread making on a garage forecourt or in the supermarket car park. The Focus then nosed through a gate to the beginning of the stage, and was gone to the furious sound of unleashed power and churning wheels. Petter Solberg, who would be on driving duty the following day, watched and listened, his head cocked to one side. Every now and then the rasping engine would become more audible, and fade again. Suddenly, like an advancing tornado, the noise was louder and the Focus, throwing up a halo of dust, became visible on the crest. It plunged down what served as a finishing straight and braked violently just before the gate. Panting like a big cat returned from the hunt, the Focus made for the shade of its lair.

An excited co-driver emerged from the lair with tales of wonder and exhilaration, a scene to be repeated throughout the day. Those who had done this kind of thing before marvelled at the economy of McRae's driving, the absolute assurance of his technique. The novices took off their helmets to reveal glaring eyes the size of golf balls, or let out shrills of delirium.

And then came the author's moment of truth More fumbling with the helmet strap. McRae climbed out for another natter with some of his crew, while others changed the tyres. A mechanic held up one of the replaced tyres, showing strands of canvas. 'He'll be able to go for it now,' someone said gleefully. 'You're lucky the weather's cleared up.' The man adjusting the five-belt harness chuckled as he gave it a final tug.

'Hi, Colin.' The offer of a handshake seemed a smart move.

'How you doin'?'

'Fine,' (Just fine, honest. Perhaps we could get this over with? In your own time, of course. Take as long as you wish.)

Since an engineer still had his head through the other window here was a chance to look at the car from the inside. Behind the driver and co-driver, where you expect to see back seats, much of the 40 metres of steel tubing that makes up the safety cage is in view, like a model of Spaghetti Junction. That strange rod with a white knob on the end, sticking out from the right side of the steering wheel, is the gear lever. Both seats have high backs and the driver, on the left, sits slightly higher than his navigator. This navigator did not plan too much navigating, and as for managing that dash-top computer ... This was surely designed for inter-galactic travel. It is difficult to identify any remnant from the road car. The indicators perhaps?

McRae is as comfortable with left-hand drive as he is left-foot braking. 'You get used to it and it's no problem at all. I've been driving like this for years.'

So the intercom works, but who wants to be holding a conversation OUT THERE?

'Are you right?'

'Y-E-A-H.' The cool approach seemed a good idea at the time.

Another cranking confirmation of reverse, then forward through the gate, and off. Except that the first 100 years – that should be yards – after the gate was not part of the stage at all. The stage started at the corner, with a ferocious snap and surge. McRae's hands and feet were instantly into well practised motion. It was neither frenzied nor casual; quick but rhythmic. All the old tips rushed around in the head. 'You know you're all right

McRae at the office.

around the bends if you can see the trees ahead and the road through the side window ... Don't panic until you're looking through the back window.'

The acceleration and braking were staggering. And the speed he was able to carry through the corners. This was no Mickey Mouse stage. The variety of the corners and gradients made it feel like an authentic test. The trees, just a few feet from the road, were certainly real. So were those logs, piled even closer to the road. And those people standing on top. Where did THEY come from? And most real of all was the endless drop at the edge of the final bend. Mercifully, there was no time to take a close look. None of these hazards appeared to even register with the driver. He negotiated every one almost as if on automatic pilot. He was still sawing at the wheel, working at that weird gear-lever, dancing on the pedals. And there was inevitable jerking and buffeting to endure. But the slalom was always controlled, the rear end always sliding to his command.

> **You get in with these drivers and realise they're in a different world**

His arms, gently bent, were static only for the final descent, an explosion of mechanical force and a rush of human adrenalin propelling the Focus to the line at 100mph. And this was a rough gravel track of barely a car and a half's width. A slam of the brakes and the panting cat plodded back to its lair again.

'OK?'

'Y-E-A-H,' Well, actually, no. Not OK. More brilliant. Absolutely, mind-blowingly brilliant. You think you can drive. You think you've seen enough of these guys to know what it's about. And then you get in with them and realise they are in a different world, a different universe. Perhaps the aliens really have landed.

And then comes the real sickener, when you ask him how much he was putting into that.

'Oh, about 70, maybe 80 per cent.'

That really does it. So much in hand, so much more to come. That extra 20 to 30 per cent might have justified the indemnity form. It would also have necessitated the trademark use of every inch of the road. But even at 70, maybe 80 per cent, McRae is a mightily impressive chauffeur.

The baying reception committee couldn't wait to open the door for the trembling wreck. 'How's the heart? ... Where's your lunch? ... Can you walk? ... Can you talk?'

They were transparently devastated to be told everything was in working order and that lunch was where it had been before the run. But, they protested, he had just produced his best time of the day: 2min 51.76sec. And not even feeling a little queasy?

Not even a blip or a tremor. The fact is it was a joy from start to finish because he was so obviously in charge throughout. This is what he does and he is known to do it exceedingly well.

McRae welcomed Martin Whitaker alongside him with particular relish. Jimmy McRae called over to his son: 'Once he's strapped in, negotiate a few more deals.' New deals or not, Colin went round in 2min 49.92sec. That is an average speed of 57.85mph. The winner's average speed on the 1999 Acropolis was 58.93mph. The fastest rally is Finland, where the winner's average speed in 1998 was 72.73mph.

Wilson surveyed all with a permanent smirk. 'Did you notice that drop from the top there?'

'NOTICE it.'

'And none of this armco stuff that the namby-pamby Formula One boys have.'

Noticed that, too. But perhaps Wilson would like a ride with his charge?

'No thanks. I don't like being a passenger. And I certainly wouldn't tell him what to do.'

During a break in the schedule, McRae gave his assessment of the stage: 'Parts of it are very rough but the best parts are good. M-Sport use this and two or three other stages up here for testing. At this time of the year they're not much help to us as far as the RAC is concerned. It needs to be later in the year, and wetter. Then you learn something from it.'

Wilson believes the exercise provided an insight into McRae's advanced driving style and the technical progress achieved by the Focus WRC.

'What you begin to appreciate when you're in the car is how Colin has changed as a driver and how the cars have changed,' he said. 'Colin has become more controlled and relaxed in his driving. He's not fighting it as much as he used to. That comes with experience and learning, but it is also down to the car. His hands are not as frantic as they used to be in the Subaru because this car is different, it's easier to drive.'

McRae concurred: 'The cars today are definitely easier to drive than they were three or four years ago. But I don't think that takes anything away from the driver. It's not as though it's all technology now. We don't have traction control or anything like that. You still get the satisfaction when you know you've driven a good stage.'

Reverting to a normal road car – let's say, the Focus road car – must be a tad tedious for McRae and the rest. Presumably he prefers something more exotic anyway?

'I actually think the Focus is a very good road car.'

There's a good company man speaking.

'No, honestly, I mean it. I think it's nice to drive, well designed, decent space, and safe. I'm happy for Alison to drive it with Hollie in there. I've never really gone in for fancy cars or expensive toys generally. Mind you, I have to admit I've just got a Ferrari 355. I've no idea what it'll do because I've not had a chance to try it properly. Well, you can't really can you?'

Oh no, of course not. But what about all that extreme sports stuff?

'I don't do that so much now because there isn't really time. But when I can I like to get out on the bike. Sometimes before the RAC I get Tommi out with me. We both get a lot of fun out of that. Gets

The final descent on the Cumbrian test stage.

us away from everything. I still enjoy skiing when I get the chance, but there are so few free days left in a year now. You've got 14 rallies, which I think is too many, from January to November, all the testing and then there are certain commitments with Ford, the commercial and corporate side of things, such as this media day, and you have to fit in the training as well. I don't enjoy jogging but I do enjoy cycling, and you have to do something you enjoy to get anything out of it. So you're killing two birds with one stone there.'

Talking of stones, what about the calorie counting? For some reason, that brought a flicker of a grin.

'We do stick to a diet leading up to events and on events,' he said. 'We're fairly strict on that.'

But what about the bacon sandwiches and the chocolate bars?

'Aye,' he acknowledged with a wider grin. 'I have to sneak them in. I've got a secret stash. We don't go to McDonald's and the fish and chip shop every day. We do eat sensibly. But now and again there's nothing wrong with having a cheeseburger, or a fry-up, or a few beers. Keeps you sane.'

Perhaps it is a healthy sign the spirit of the young rebel is still alive inside this maturing family man. The spirit must never be incarcerated. It must be free to fire the competitive instinct, to generate motivation.

'You have to keep up your motivation if you want to be successful. You see some guys go on till they're 40 and as long as they've got the motivation that's fine. My motivation is certainly still there. I feel I've still got a lot of winning to do. I want to win at least one more Championship, maybe two. I've got another year on this contract and I'll probably look for an-

'Bikes are for fun!'

other two years after that. Maybe that will be enough. I don't want to go on and on for the sake of it. Ideally you want to finish at the top.'

And when he has finished World Championship rallying, will he find another avenue for his competitive spirit? Could he even give Formula One a try?

'Whenever I compete I want to compete at my best. I couldn't do anything half-hearted. That's why motorbike racing is a non-starter. I've survived this far! Bikes are for fun, not racing. Perhaps touring cars, but more likely GT. I'd want the real power. I'm looking forward to driving Ford's Grand Prix car. I drove a Jordan a few years ago. But I'm not serious about Formula One. That was a good story at the time. Having said that, if I'm a second a lap quicker than Johnny Herbert ... Anyway, I'm not the type of person who likes all the hype and high profile of the Formula One stars. I wouldn't like any more attention than I get. That all makes it harder. I'm sure it gets to guys like Michael Schumacher and Damon Hill. It's enough having to cope with what I have.'

The movement towards neatly packaged, standardised, televised rallies should make bigger stars of the leading rally drivers. McRae has firm views on the development of his sport.

'The television side of it needs to be sorted, and if Bernie Ecclestone [head of FIA's marketing operation and the man credited with making Formula One the global attraction it is today] really gets into it then there's every chance that will happen. Super special stages are OK if they are good ones, like Australia. It's also at the end of the day in Australia, which makes it better. I think three points for a super special stage win is too much, though. The rallies need to be standardised, so viewers know when they can see them, just like grands prix. The other thing to look at is the running order in a rally. I think the idea of giving the top six guys the choice of running order is a good one. That way you are rewarded rather than handicapped for a good day, just as you are in Formula One qualifying.'

Of more immediate concern was the remainder of the 1999 season and his quest for the Championship.

'We've still got a chance because nobody's running away with it, and we know we have a car with the potential to win rallies and a team to get the job done. Obviously we have to start winning rallies soon if we're going to do it this year but if not we should have a great chance next year. That's what drives you on.'

chapter nine

Squad game

You hear it applied to just about every sport now: It's a squad game. The days of straightforward 11-a-side seem as distant as England at the vanguard of world football and cricket. Rotation systems and horses for courses are the order of the day. For that you need cover in every position and team players with manageable egos. Ford adopted the concept for their World Rally Championship operation in an endeavour not only to support Colin McRae and the main thrust of their attack, but also to nurture talent for the future.

Co-drivers are squad players by definition and function. They provide for the driver and rarely receive public recognition, let alone acclaim, for their contribution. However, Nicky Grist happens to be the one other member of the Ford Martini squad scheduled for a full programme of rallies. Thomas Rådström, Simon Jean-Joseph, Petter Solberg, Fred Gallagher and Phil Mills all knew they would have to take their turn on the bench.

If that distinction has given Grist an inflated opinion of himself it does not show. In fact he appears more inclined towards self-deprecation than self-aggrandisement. He assumes no influence over McRae other than to guide him through stages as quickly and safely as possible. McRae appreciates that, just as he appreciates the levity the little Welshman offers through the long and often laborious necessity of recces, covering the same ground three times to compile the most accurate possible pace notes.

'Generally Colin sorts himself out,' Grist says modestly. 'We've got a very good professional, working relationship. I'm there if he wants me, if he needs someone to lift him when things aren't going right. But there comes a time when you have to leave him to think about things and I just go away. I don't really act as a counsellor to him. Colin is the kind of guy who makes his own mind up about things. I just do my job. If he respects it then that's good.'

McRae has confirmed as much, but precisely what makes a good co-driver requires some explanation.

'Obviously a fairly good nerve,' Grist confesses reassuringly. 'Preparation is very important. You have to make sure you've thought of everything. And you have to pull people together. Co-drivers have a lot to do when they come in at the end of a stage and at the end of the day. Sometimes you can finish a stage and go and have something to eat, but generally there are always things to do. Things like

A touch of bonding for McRae, Grist, Jean-Joseph and Gallagher.

MARTINI
MARTINI
RACING
MARTINI
RACING
MARTINI
RACING
MICHELIN
MARTINI

checking the fuel consumption, making sure I've worked it out right. And the tactics, talking it over with the team, deciding what we do next.

'What really helps at all times is a cool head. You are in a very tense situation in that office, out on a stage. We spend the majority of the time in there together. I'm on the pace notes, he's driving, and no matter how well prepared you may be, things can go wrong, things can break. You have to try and turn negative things around. That's part of the job, too. But nothing makes up for retirement on a rally. You can never really accept it and get used to it. Scoring points and winning rallies is what it's all about.'

You're aware of not only the danger to yourself but also to others

Low scoring and winning golf tournaments is what it used to be all about for the young Grist, back in his home town of Abergavenny. He might have been another Ian Woosnam, although he concedes that was never likely.

'I started golf young but not young enough,' he says. 'I was about 11. It was such a big part of my life. In fact it was my whole life. Any spare time I had in the summer, in the evenings and at weekends, I'd always be down at the golf club. Eventually I got a job teaching golf, semi-pro. But then I got interested in motorsport and I went spectating on a few road rallies. They started at midnight on Saturday and went through to daybreak on Sunday. I got into navigating. I couldn't afford to get my own car and drive so I always did the navigating.

'It got to the point where I had to decide between golf and rallying because I was working Saturday and Sunday at the golf club and doing the rallies at night. The rallying was getting better so I decided to go for that and get a normal day job. As it happens I went into the motor trade. My golf pro used to say to me, "You want to pack in this rallying, there'll never be any money in it." It was a great feeling to go back 12 or 13 years later and hear him say, "I'll eat my words now."

'It's a good life. It's obviously not as fruitful as the drivers' but at the end of the day the advantage of being a co-driver is that you do lead your own life when you're away from the rallying. The drivers get pestered pillar to post. Poor Colin, I can see how he feels. I can imagine being in his position and feeling exactly the same. I know they are well paid and everything, but you need a private life. Co-drivers can go home, relax and live normally. You need that when you're away for something like nine months of the year.'

McRae may be the driver, the superstar with the mega-buck salary, but Grist is subjected to the same emotional and psychological roller-coaster ride, wrestling with the same fears and facing the same potential perils.

'You're conscious of not only the dangers to yourselves but also to others, to spectators and photographers,' Grist says. 'Anybody who is familiar with the safety precautions in Formula One is staggered by what they see on some rallies. If someone even tip-toes on the grass at a grand prix all hell is let loose. But in rallying it's always been like this. Having said that, it's 100 per cent better now than it ever has been.

'It's something you have to come to terms with. You're there to perform. You can't think about these things because if you do you're going to be much slower. It doesn't matter what kind of motorsport you do, if you thought too much about the consequences of any accident you would never be able to do it.

'My worst accident was with Juha Kankkunen on the 1994 Safari. A big washaway appeared on the road and we managed to jump over it with the front of the car but the back crashed out and we went end over end. It was a major drama. I was lucky I had just a few cuts and bruises and was a bit shaken up.'

Kankkunen recalls the incident equally vividly. They were travelling at 190kph when they were caught out by the water, a metre deep, which gushed on to the road

Nicky Grist's pace notes – competitive section 8 Safari Rally

CS8 – Morendat to Mbaruk

The top left hand corner gives me the length of this section, which helps if we have a problem or if Colin needs to know how far it is to the end of the stage.

The top right hand corner gives me the page number we are on (3) and the total number of pages for this section (29).

The next line explains, to our gravel crew and myself, the exact location of the start of the section, which in this case is 50 metres after the railway crossing.

Notes: 250, 70, 300, etc. are the distances of the straight between each instruction. Corners: These explain to Colin the speed, line, length, if it opens or tightens, any crests and any additional information such as narrow bridges with cares and cautions for the tricky or dangerous places along the way.

The corners are described with a number system which relates to the gears and, of course, L = left and R = right. The page illustrated reads as follows:

250 long six left tightens to minus ('long sixth gear left which tightens' – in this case it would mean a lift off the throttle at the minus); 70 four right tightens ('tightens' by itself means to keep in on exit); 300 crest and right tightens to five plus opens (describes a slight right corner which then tightens to fifth gear on throttle [+] and then it opens which tells him the road widens on exit.) 'Slow' is another speed which in the case of the two on this page is fourth gear. A '!' is a care, meaning to watch this one because what follows is a third gear corner over a narrow bridge. A crest with a six underneath explains that this is flat out over it. The numbers underneath this bridge are for my information only. The '2' is the roadbook junction number and the distance is how far it is from the start.

Grist runs through his Safari pace notes.

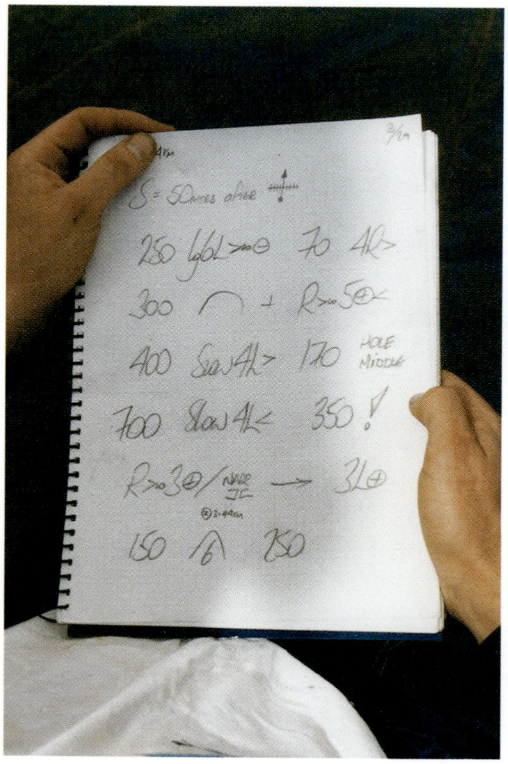

after torrential rain. Their car was tossed into a crazy, rotating momentum for 100 metres. Kankkunen's helmet took the brunt of the battering and he was unhurt.

Grist resumes: 'Of course I am aware we can have accidents and hurt ourselves. I can't say I'm not. I must say the one we could have had on the Acropolis this year would have been very nasty. There are times when you can see something coming, you have a bit of a moment and it's like, "Ooh, wow." My reaction is to grab the seat with one hand. But your mind has to be totally focused on the pace notes because if Colin doesn't get the information we're going to be in trouble anyway. You just take it as it comes.

'The good thing now is that while World Championship rallying is getting faster, the technical regulations and the safety regulations of the cars have improved dramatically. The cars today are far safer than they've ever been. If you have an accident you expect to get out. We have an integral roll-cage, all welded together, and very strong. My biggest fear, as I suppose it is for most people, is going sideways into a tree. Unlike racing, where if you go off you have run-off areas, into barriers and tyre walls, in rallying you are faced with absolutely anything.

'But then when you're with a top-line driver you feel that bit more secure. Although he's going much, much faster than most other people, his ability is so much greater than most other people's, and it's surprising what they can do with a car. One day it may happen, but it may not. Best not to think about it.'

He's not working hard, not fighting it – he's just flowing

No disrespect to the boss, Malcolm Wilson, with whom Grist had his first full-time professional contract, or Kankkunen, his Championship-winning partner, but he has encountered a new dimension with McRae.

'I think he's just got this natural ability,' Grist says. 'He's not trying to make things happen or force them, they happen with him just going through the motions. He's not working hard, he's not fighting it. He's just flowing. When you look at some of the other drivers, say Carlos Sainz or Didier Auriol – and don't get me wrong, they are very fast rally drivers – they don't seem so natural as Colin, or Juha Kankkunen for that matter. The car is like putty in Colin's hands. He can do anything with it and yet he isn't putting stress on the car. That's the impressive thing. And what makes Colin even more special is the ability to dig deeper and get that extra five to ten seconds when he has to. That's what makes the great rally driver. I think Tommi Mäkinen is maybe the only other driver in the Championship who can do that.

'Colin has certainly come on a lot over the last few years. I think he always used the throttle before the brain but now he applies the brain a lot more. He has matured and that makes him very clever. He knows when to back off, what to do in any given situation. We got caught out on the Acropolis where the others slowed and for the first time we found ourselves in a position we didn't want to be on the second morning. We were leading the rally and first on the road. But after two-and-a-half years that's not bad going and he's getting better at the strategical side all the time.

'People often ask how he compares with the top Formula One guys or how he would go in Formula One. Of course, it's difficult to say because they are completely different forms of motorsport, but I would say that given a couple of months' testing Colin would be bloody quick on a race circuit, whereas most Formula One drivers would still be getting to grips with a rally car. Having seen Schumacher in the wet, I'd say he'd be bloody good in a rally car because he's not worried about that Formula One car sliding. I think he's the one who compares with Colin. The others are all straight line guys.

'I do enjoy sitting alongside Colin and appreciate what he does, but it can get to the stage where you take it for granted. People want to know what it's like and ask about certain things, and I can say, "I never noticed that." It's just a job now. I'd love to be able to drive like Colin, I must admit. I wouldn't mind driving a rally one day, but I wouldn't have a chance in hell of matching Colin. When you see the guy fully lit he really is very special. You know when he's really trying, you can feel it. The notes come that much quicker and on every corner he's teetering on the edge of going off the road.'

Which is why Grist harbours not a shred of envy. However, he is satisfied he plays a crucial role in the squad game, and that McRae recognises as much.

'The driver is the guy who's pushing the pedals and steering, but I think most other people don't understand that without those pace notes he loses 20 to 25 per cent of his pace straightaway. That's the difference between first or second and 10th or 11th. It really is that dramatic. They are the guys who are up front all the time, they are the guys who get all the media attention. But we are the guys who are behind the scenes, sorting out the car, having a very big input into the result. And when we finish a rally and we've won it I think, "Yes, great, I've done it," and I can enjoy it and get satisfaction from it just as much as the driver can.'

At the age of 37 Grist believes he is still fit enough and ambitious enough to anticipate a few more Championship campaigns, but he is already contemplating life beyond the navigator's seat.

'I suppose I'll go on as long as Colin, or somebody else, wants me to co-drive for them and I'm getting a full-time contract. But I don't think I'd want to go on too long into my forties. You've got to look at slowing down some time in life. I've seen some co-drivers around until they're 50 but I'm sure it must be getting hard for them and I wouldn't fancy that. I don't think I'd want to work in any other capacity in a team after co-driving. I wouldn't want to be a manager or anything like that.

'I wouldn't mind doing some commentating. I think rallying needs that. Rallying is going through a great change as far as TV is concerned and there is a place for a Martin Brundle type of figure to do what he has done for Formula One, taken it to that next level. I read some reports and I think, "You've missed the point, it's not like that." There's no reason why rallying shouldn't go from strength to strength, as Formula One has.'

In the meantime, Grist has unfinished business, and here he identifies a fundamental difference between the two motorsport disciplines.

'For rally drivers it's all about endurance and stamina over three days. With Formula One it's concentrating the mental and physical effort into one-and-a-half hours of a grand prix. So the endurance type of training is more impor-

Who says there's no glamour in co-driving?

tant for us. A lot of these guys today are super slim and super fit. If you are going to stretch yourself like a professional cyclist or a marathon runner you have to put a lot of effort into it, and I can see the benefits of that. But we can still be human. We can go and have a few beers and steak and chips afterwards. We're happy with our fitness levels. We know we have to do it for three or three-and-a-half days, and we can.'

Thomas Rådström and Fred Gallagher have been the most active second pairing in the team, with similarly mixed fortunes, satisfactions and frustrations. For all the talk of long-term planning and laying foundations, Rådström had by necessity to apply a keener sense of urgency to his work. He was no youngster. Time was not on his side. He joined on a one-year contract and could not afford to waste a minute of his scheduled rallies. Breaking his leg just before the Safari was a cruel trick of fate. But he has remained defiantly optimistic, drawing encouragement from evidence of progress and accepting the disappointments philosophically.

Ford is one of the biggest, most serious, professional rally teams

'It's always pressure when you are a works driver,' he says. 'You need a couple of rallies to learn the team. I was with Toyota for a long time and knew everybody there, but this year everything has been new – the car, engineers, mechanics, their names, everything. It's difficult. Then when I broke my leg I had to miss two rallies and it put me back because you need kilometres in the car before you are up to speed again.

'I slipped after what was nothing more than a very late lunch with the other boys and it was really hard to fly home from Kenya with a broken leg. I was thinking about my future and I was in pain. I didn't know how badly it was broken and how long it would take. I was alone on the plane and it was one of the worst times of my life. When I went to the toilet it was not possible to close the door. I had to have one leg outside. It was hard.

'When I came back I did two days' testing in Argentina and it went quite well. I was surprised. In Greece it was disappointing because we were in the lead and then had to retire. At least I was up to speed again. But you need to finish rallies and be consistent. You have to be realistic also and remember who you are competing against. Almost all have more experience than I have on every rally. But when I put my helmet on I don't think of that. I just go flat out as possible.

'I wish to stay at Ford. That is what I am working for, to do a full season with Ford. It is one of the biggest, most serious and professional teams. You see how serious they are in Formula One as well as this rally business. Toyota are big as well but this is even a little more serious. I know there are drivers in front of me for the drive but I cannot do more than try to do my best.

'It is good for me to have Fred. He does a fantastic job in the car, he is a good guy, and when you are in an English team it helps to have an English co-driver. He knows more people than I do and some in the team have this dialect, and when you are on the radio and everybody is a bit up it can be tricky to understand exactly every word. So sometimes he is like a translator. I am improving my English but it's good to have Fred with me.'

Gallagher, born in Northern Ireland and resident in Scotland, has learned to cope with drivers' slips. Many co-drivers subscribe to the view that if drivers were any good at geography they would not require navigators. Despite his many and disparate adventures, Gallagher has revelled in this unexpected assignment.

'Having moved from the World Championship to rally raids I thought that was it,' he confesses. 'I'd decided my rallying career was finished, and then Bruno Thiry broke his ribs last year in Kenya, Ari was asked to do the rally and I joined him. We did Portugal, then Finland and I still didn't expect any more of it, but Malcolm phoned me towards the autumn, asked if I would go with Thomas and we agreed.

'Then, by a series of coincidences, Petter Solberg was introduced to me and I had a look at him. I phoned Malcolm and he said I should sit with him on a test. Simon Jean-Joseph was over with his manager the same day and I also co-drove with him. I'd learned a fair bit of French, working for Citroën for seven years. So I started the season with Simon, then got the first podium with Thomas in Sweden. When Thomas broke his leg I ended up with Petter on the Safari and we did the recce in an old rented Jeep, which was pretty hopeless. We went to the shakedown and I could see the red mist over his eyes. He drove off at a million miles an hour, smacking rocks here and there. I was trying to talk to him but there wasn't any listening going on. We finally broke three wheels and couldn't go any further.

'We went back and Malcolm was furious with him, and we had a fairly interesting 30-minute meeting. Malcolm basically told me I could slap him, anything I wanted, to control him. I could even turn the master switch off if he drove too quickly. And I have to say he drove very sensibly after that. Even when it looked as if we were going to finish eighth or ninth he just kept the same pace up. He's a clever guy and seems to be a quick driver. You can never tell 100 per cent but he's looking good.

'Rallying has changed very much in the time I've been involved. These days there are very few differences in the regulations. It used to be very important to get the regulations for, say, the Acropolis, and read through to see what little differences they had. Now we have standard regulations. We also used to have free servicing, so you would always be looking after your

Even a navigator as experienced as Gallagher can be driven to distraction.

time and working out where you might gain advantage. These days you have service parks and you've got 20 minutes in there. The other change is that practice used to be pretty much free so we would go over a stage between five and ten times, whereas now it's limited to two or three. But when people talk about the "good old days" there were really only Peugeot and Lancia in it. Today we have … what is it? … eight manufacturers.

'On rally raids I used to think to myself sometimes "what the hell am I doing here?" I had some scary moments, rolling tail over nose. The fire incident on the Safari wasn't that bad. We were at a service point and had the engine running. A young mechanic, who happened to be called Guenther Steiner, dropped a can of fuel on the rear brake disc. Flames went under the car and Bjorn pulled me out of his side. My heart was thumping for a while and I got a little burnt. I keep saying to Guenther, "You're the man who tried to kill me!" Malcolm winds him up as well, telling him he didn't put that on his cv.

You always want the chance to get off the bench and do a bit more

'I've been very lucky to have been with a lot of world champions, but I've enjoyed this year enormously. A guy like Colin doesn't need a lot of help from his co-driver aside from the notes because he has the confidence and the experience, whereas the three guys I've been with maybe don't have that total self-confidence yet. So I try to help them in any way I can. The main problem I have is remembering which language to speak when I get in the car. If Ford offered me another year I think I would do it with Thomas and then maybe think about stopping. It's a bit late to start thinking about moving to other teams. I'm quite happy here.'

Jean-Joseph, the tarmac man, has had to condense still more emotional and physical energy into his opportunities. If some spills over, it is understandable.

'It has all been very exciting for me,' he says. 'To be involved in this project has been a great experience for me. I never expected the car to be so fast so early in its life and for me that makes it a real pleasure to be part of the team. As well as learning about a new car and team this year, I have also had to learn a lot about the World Rally Championship because I had competed on only two Championship events before this year.

'I am still very much learning about competing at this level. The main objective for me now is to develop further my knowledge and continue to work with the team to develop the tarmac potential of the Focus.'

Of all the squad players Solberg is the least known quantity and perhaps the joker in the pack. Wilson is backing a hunch with the young Norwegian and if he has half the success Richards had with the fledgling McRae he will be entitled to consider it an inspired move. Solberg's youthful enthusiasm is as apparent as his impatience to be summoned from the bench. He shares the same conviction as his countryman, Ole Gunnar Solskjaer, the Manchester United footballer, that when he is pressed into service he can deliver. But first of all, back to that day in Cumbria. What was he listening for as McRae drove away in the Focus?

'The engine. The sound is incredible. I try to listen to everything because I like cars and I work a lot with cars. So it's very important to listen.'

Solberg has a lot of listening and learning to do.

'For sure. This is a great chance for me. I have a five-year contract and time to do things, but you always want to do things more and more, and do things faster. It is the same for me as it is for Solskjaer. You always want the chance to get off the bench and do a bit more. I want to be out there. I want it so much.'

Rarely can there have been a more dramatic substitution than Solberg's introduction as replacement for Rådström on the Safari.

'Yeah, incredible,' Solberg says with a still disbelieving shake of his blond head.

'I should have been on a rally in Norway, driving an Escort. Then I got a phone call at about nine o'clock in the evening from Malcolm, saying I had to leave for Kenya the following morning and start the recce to drive on the Safari. I said, "Have you had something to drink or something?" He said no, he was serious. I couldn't believe it for five or ten minutes. The Safari! The biggest and toughest rally. For sure, it was a big vote of confidence.

'And then I realised I had to get the tickets and everything, and started to work out how I was going to do that. It was quite a tough job because it was so late at night and I had to leave at seven o'clock the following morning. Eventually I got the tickets sorted and set off to the airport in Oslo to find a hotel. I didn't want to risk leaving home in the morning and getting held up by bad weather. I tried three hotels but they were all full, so as it was now three o'clock in the morning I just went into the airport, sat down on a bench and slept there.

'On the rally I had to be careful, just as on all the rallies I have been on. I finished my first three in the World Championship for Ford, with the Escort in Sweden and with the Focus on the Safari and Portugal, so that was good. Also because they are two totally different cars and I had two different co-drivers.

'To finish fifth on Safari was great. You couldn't believe it because it was so rough and such a long rally. But I had Fred with me and he was good for me. That helped a lot. I know he was told to hit me if I did not behave myself but I could always hit back! What I have to do is make a good job with the rallies I have left this year and hopefully I'll have ten rallies next year. That is the plan but we have to wait and see.

'It is difficult to slow down your natural style because it makes you more nervous. My style is not aggressive but I like to be fast. On tarmac it is important to

Jean-Joseph, on a steep learning curve.

have a rhythm in the car. It is difficult to get into that natural rhythm when you don't want to take chances. I have to learn the notes much better also. It is all about learning.

'That's why it is good for me to be with Colin. I talk to him about different things, the set-up of the car, especially on jumps and stuff. "How do you do that?" I ask him. You have to try these things. He is the best. He has a lot of confidence. He has been driving for many years. He has a good car and a good team, he has good notes, a good co-driver, everything is there. Everything has to fit to get it right.'

Things have started to fit for Solberg in a way he could not have envisaged until he had the initiative to send that video for Wilson's consideration. The test provided him with the opportunity he required.

My whole family, my whole village, 200 people, went crazy that day – it was enormous

'It was unbelievable and very emotional when I got the job,' he recalls. 'I had been testing with other drivers on the Thursday and on the Saturday the team had a meeting to discuss what they were going to do. On the Sunday morning I got a call from Malcolm. He told me they were giving me a three-year contract. Then, a couple of days later, they called me again and said they wanted to make it five years.

'Well, my whole family, my whole village, 200 people, went crazy that day. It was enormous. There was television, the media, everything. My mother was crying she was so happy, everybody was so happy. My mother and father had driven and they knew how much this meant. My brother and I have been working on rally cars since we were nine and ten years old. It was always rallying for me. Now rallying is the biggest thing over there.'

Solberg is pretty big, too. Commercial cardboard cut-outs have appeared on garage forecourts, testifying to his celebrity status and the marketability of the 'Hollywood' image. Wilson, who had taken him under his management wing, can be expected to ensure his protégé does not get star-struck on the back of a few bit parts. Solberg acknowledges he has to earn top billing.

'I can't really think of what I can do for rallying in Norway and how many drivers will come from my country in future. I have to think of myself and how to get the best out of myself. I have not really done anything yet. I have to concentrate on my work at Ford. I obviously would like to think I could be Colin's full-time teammate in the future. The plan is to get a full contract. But for the moment I just want to drive more, and learn and improve.

'I feel I have come to the right team for that. It is more like a family than a team. I don't know what the other teams are like but this team makes you feel so welcome and part of it. I just hope I can do the job for them and for me. I want that so much.

'Long term, of course the World Championship is the plan. It has to be if you are ambitious and want to fulfil yourself. I feel that is a possibility for me. I know I have time on my side, but I want to get there quickly. That's why it's not easy to sit and wait.'

Phil Mills has had to contend with similar constraints. At the age of 36 he still prefers the navigator's seat to the day job.

'My work is a nice combination,' says the man from mid-Wales. 'It's lovely to be involved with a team, especially in the coordination department, but the co-driving is my first love. I do the office job to do the co-driving. There's nothing like the buzz of being in the car and I want to do that for another ten years. Then I'll want to slip into the management role, which is why I have to keep in touch with the other side of the business.

'Our programme this year has been limited. Next year we're hoping to do a minimum of ten rallies, in which case the office side of things is going to be very difficult, if not impossible, especially with fitness programmes now coming into co-driving. That takes up four hours a day.

'Petter is certainly an interesting boy. You have to keep reminding yourself how young he is. And he's a bit of a character.

The sport needs people like that. His talent is unquestionable. He's a bit short of mileage and this year has obviously been a culture shock to him. He's been around the world twice and done the recce on every rally except Argentina to get the whole picture in his head.

'He took the decision quite early on to do all his work in English. His English isn't 100 per cent but he's been working with the team as much as he can and goes to the tests, all of which will help him improve. Most of the top drivers, the Kankkunens and so on, do their notes in English and Petter wanted to do the same. Sometimes he says my English is too perfect and he has to listen a bit harder than normal. You just have to be clear and precise and emphasise things a little more than you would with an English driver.

'We use a number system for the notes. We grade corners one to six and almost invariably you find a "four right" will be a fourth gear corner and a "one right" a hairpin. Every driver has a different system and this is the one he likes. It's the easiest. Like all other drivers, even Tommi Mäkinen, he's changing little things on his notes all the time. Drivers' notes are evolving constantly. Petter's notes eight months on from Monte Carlo were almost completely different. They have been getting better and as the speeds increase we are taking a lot of the finer detail out and leaving more important things in a shorter call.

'It's a little bit frustrating holding back on rallies because if you are a co-driver or driver you are a competitive person, and you know you could have been X seconds quicker on the stage if you'd gone a bit harder. But there's no secret about the team orders. He's got a five-year programme and nobody's had that before. He's a lucky guy. The first year he learns and finishes every rally. The second year he goes a little quicker but still finishes every rally. The third year he goes a bit quicker again and maybe takes the odd chance. The fourth year he adds quite a lot of speed and the fifth year we go for it.

'I was employed to do the job on that basis and you have to be professional and accept that. In Portugal he drove with incredible reserve and I was very impressed with the way he coped with that situation. He was told in no uncertain terms he had to take the car to the finish. There's no reason why he can't go to the top, and I'd like to be there with him.'

By mid-season 1999 the Ford Martini team were reassessing not only the development of the car but also their driver squad system. Malcolm Wilson and Martin Whitaker had more serious talking to do.

Whitaker revealed the train of thought:

Solberg, a star in the making.

Mills
14
Solberg
Ford
SWEDISH RALLY
ERICSSON
14
NIKKO
office
Valvoline
NIKKO
Ford

Solberg and Mills believe they are heading in the right direction to realise their dreams.

'We made a commitment to aim at 2000 for the Championship and it makes sense to go for both titles. To achieve that we need a more established base and better continuity. That means two full-time drivers. It's fair to say the Drivers' Championship is the one that carries the more kudos, but to win that you have to have a strong driver line-up. We always knew our tactic of having three drivers was an unusual course, but we had a lot of work to do on the car and therefore it probably served its purpose in part. Two strong drivers push each other, and if you can get one of them ahead and the other scoring points on a regular basis he's taking points off other people.'

To that end Ford had discussions with Tommi Mäkinen, champion for the previous three years and current title leader. McRae rose publicly to the potential challenge. 'That way we'll find out which one of us is the quicker,' he said. Pay represented another possible hurdle. Having won three times as many Championships as the Scot, Mäkinen would not be likely to join the team on a lower retainer.

Whitaker said: 'Colin doesn't have a problem about the other driver. It really doesn't affect him. He does want to make sure we are in a position to run equal cars to the same levels and standards of competitiveness, but that's no more than you would expect him to want. As far as the money is concerned you've got to be careful you don't go completely crazy. The investment we made in Colin was for the right reasons. You've got to look at every driver on his merits but at the same time make sure things don't spiral out of control.'

Jean-Joseph was told he would not be in contention for a place in Ford's World Championship team for 2000 but Rådström had the opportunity to stake his claim.

Wilson said: 'We have spoken to Tommi but so have other teams. Some people say it would be fireworks to put Colin and Tommi together, but it would be spectacular. You've got to keep pushing for the very best. You've got to have a go. That obviously comes at a price and I wouldn't insult Tommi by offering him less than Colin. But Thomas certainly still has a chance and he's got three or four more rallies to show what he can do.'

chapter ten

Long and winding road

The schedule relented at last after the Acropolis, a five-week gap before the Rally of New Zealand offering the opportunity to take breath if not a break. The cycle of testing, developing and more testing is unending; a vicious, all-consuming circle; a tantalising, elusive rotation which can never settle on perfection.

For the Ford Martini team the delay in competitive action provided the chance to reappraise a campaign that was supposed now to be accelerating instead of stuttering. Success came earlier than anticipated. Perhaps they were spoiled. Certainly their expectations were raised. They now believed the Championship was still within range, but they had to start winning again. And soon. Preferably in New Zealand. It is the longest trip on the tour, yet having come this far Ford were in no mood to retreat.

'We're still in a good position for the Championship, with six events left,' was Wilson's studied and defiant assessment back in his haven, called Cumbria. 'We're in a far better position than we were after Sweden. We were 20 points behind then. We're 13 points behind now. We're constantly working to improve the car. Trimming the weight is an on-going process. There are so many aspects you can look at: new materials, new technology. We'll be doing that even when we get down to the minimum weight because then we'll be able to redistribute the weight to our benefit. It's been so difficult because of the weight of the initial body shell. I think all manufacturers are going to struggle with weight now because the road cars are having to be so much stronger, much stiffer and more impact-resistant.

'If you look at the remaining rallies Finland is the one that doesn't favour Colin, but from his point of view and mine, it's the one we would dearly love to win. Over the years Colin has set numerous fastest times in Finland and if he could just keep it together he could do it. It's all gravel but it's specialised, with all the big jumps, followed by blind corners. He's always had a problem there because of his flamboyant style, dropping a back wheel in a ditch, that sort of thing. He needs to adopt a less flamboyant approach. I haven't talked to him about it yet but I will do, no question. I know he's ambitious, and we all know the speed is there, but he has to show the judgement, as he did in Portugal. His drive there was sensational.

'I think Colin is at his peak from a speed point of view, and this year I've wanted him to be as hard on the car as possible because we have to get on and get it sorted. Next year is going to be the big one, so it's got to be right for 2000, otherwise the man from Ford will be knocking on my door wanting to know why it's not.

'We are going for the Championship next year and it will definitely require a little bit of a different philosophy from us, from Colin, from a lot of members of the team. We have to make sure we're right on top of the job and understand what we have to do. At the end of this year we'll sit down and have a good talk about it all, about this year and what we've learned, and how we go about next year. It will be an open and frank discussion.

'But I don't want to do that now. I want to get the car right, and Colin can be as hard as he wants on it. He'll maybe be disappointed if something else breaks, but I'd rather that happened now to help us make sure everything is sorted for next year.'

The man from Ford reiterates his faith in Wilson and does not envisage having to knock on his door.

Whitaker says: 'We've developed a long-term contract with Malcolm which goes on for a further four years. That, again, is remarkable for Ford because traditionally we haven't done contracts for that length of time. But if you are serious about something you've got to develop it for the long term. It was always my stated ambition that we were going to take Ford back to the forefront of premier motorsport competition, be it in Formula One or rallying. People who knew me, and people I talked to in the Press, thought I'd completely taken leave of my senses, because Ford had dropped off the edge of the scale in terms of competition. But it's beginning to happen.

'You've only to look at Malcolm's team – the professionalism, the presentation element and the results. We had two wins under our belt long before anyone anticipated. That, in a sense, created a problem because it raised expectations to a level we didn't really want to cope with at that time. But everything we're doing in the Ford World Championship family is moving on apace. In Formula One the purchase of Cosworth Racing and then the purchase of the Formula One team itself completes the circle. And it sends out the very strong message that Ford is serious about what it's doing.

'That will become more and more evident. As Malcolm indicates, you will see that in the rally team. Everybody will have to move up a gear. A lot of people have already moved up a gear. You only have to be with the guys in the field to see how

McRae masters the slippery stages of New Zealand before coming to a frustrating halt.

they operate and react. They are an amazing bunch of people. But we have to keep moving forward and be tough about it. There are many areas where we've got to ramp it up. Everything has to be that bit more focused. Like everything in life, you have a constant evolution, a constant raising of standards.

'The new factory is a symbol of that progress. People will work in a different way, they won't be so much on top of each other. We won't want to lose the special atmosphere the team has, because that club-like element is important. That encourages good teamwork. I think M-Sport demonstrate the value of teamwork in a very high profile way.'

There was, in the meantime, much ground still to be covered in 1999, starting with New Zealand.

Wilson said: 'It's a rally where you have to be highly committed. Colin is especially good on those long corners, where a big commitment is required. It's high-speed stuff. But we'll have to do a lot of work. You have to have good travel on your suspension, very good traction. You have to keep your wheels in contact with the road. We know what we have to do with the car, it's a matter of whether we can get it exactly to his liking.'

Rådström ultimately slides out of contention.

Rådström and McRae were second and third respectively on the opening super special stage, run on the outskirts of Auckland. Rain, floodlights and an enthusiastic crowd generated a keen atmosphere. Out on the wet roads the following morning it soon became clear the only drivers capable of setting the pace were McRae and Mäkinen. They traded fastest times and pulled away from the pack, trailering the prospect of a titanic contest.

Survival was an achievement for Rådström on that first full day. He rolled his Focus, severely rearranging the lines of the car, and dropped to tenth. 'There was a sweeping fast right-hand bend and the car slid wide,' the Swede said. 'The rear wheel clipped a bank, causing the car to flip on to its side and then on to the roof. It rolled right over and ended up back on its wheels. Fred got out to look at the damage and saw it was OK to carry on, but the car handled really badly for the rest of the stage because the impact had broken a wheel.'

Mechanically, the car was sound and Rådström continued, confident of making up lost ground. McRae reinforced the optimism in the camp with his third stage win to take the overall lead. However, 10km into the next test the Focus expired. McRae fired the engine back into life, only for it to stop again. Another rally was over prematurely for the Scot.

'It's frustrating,' he said, reflecting the mood of the entire camp. 'The car was performing so well and we'd proved we had the set-up right for these stages. We'd had problems with a misfire earlier and we thought we'd cured it, but it came back and there was nothing we could do.'

Richard Burns also made an early exit, prompting McRae to couple their plights. 'Richard and I are in the same boat and it's sinking fast.' Their Championship aspirations were not exactly sunk without trace, but the point was taken on board.

Rådström was still afloat. Sixth

overnight, he advanced to fourth the following day, carried along by the currents of three fastest stage times. Twenty kilometres into the final leg, however, he was swept off course and out of the rally, marooned in a muddy ditch, incurring the disapprobation of Gallagher. 'That's it, then,' pronounced the stern-faced co-driver.

A crestfallen Rådström said: 'It was the same route as the opening test on the first day so it was very muddy and quite badly cut up. We approached a very slow right-hand bend and slid a little wide. The car just slipped off the edge on the inside and became stuck. The nose was buried and we just couldn't push the car back on again.

'It was a bit terrible walking back. I had easily a fourth place there. But what happened was horrible for me, Malcolm and the whole team. I felt bad for everybody. But you have to keep your mood up and forget it. There's no point in thinking about it any more.'

McRae's car was a source of further exasperation, as Guenther Steiner relates: 'The mechanics went in to collect it and it started perfectly. They drove it back to the workshop in Auckland. On the day after we checked everything and couldn't find a problem. I told the boys to take it out and try it. After seven or eight kilometres it died, then picked up again and they drove it for another couple of hours. It was only when we got it back to England we discovered a cable was chafing.'

The team were reeling from a succession of punishing blows and Mäkinen's win took him 23 points clear of McRae, but the ever-resourceful Steiner mustered an optimistic note. 'We should not be frustrated because who could have expected anything like this? We can still drive for the Championship. If Tommi wins in Finland it may be over then, but if he doesn't Colin still has a chance and the rest of the season should be good for us. Having Thomas winning stages shows it's not only Colin, it's the car as well.'

* * *

All-star line-up in Finland. Back row, left to right: Armin Schwarz's Skoda; Juha Kankkunen's Subaru; François Delecour's Peugeot; Harri Rovanperä's Seat. Front row, left to right: Carlos Sainz's Toyota; Tommi Mäkinen's Mitsubishi; Colin McRae's Ford.

A confident Rådström finds his rhythm on Finland's rally of lakes and trees.

For all McRae's apprehension about Rally Finland, no event offered greater opportunity for preparation. The long summer days provided sufficient light to cram double shifts between breakfast and supper. And yet McRae, who had managed only one finish over the revered jumps, arrived in the host town of Jyvaskyla, 280 kilometres north of Helsinki, maintaining victory was an unrealistic objective. His priority was to complete the 23 stages. A place on the podium would be more than satisfactory. Wilson's fears that his No. 1 driver might be too flamboyant to negotiate this rally appeared to have been allayed.

Rådström, by contrast, declared himself confident and doubtless drew strength from the support of his fan club, all decked in tall blue and yellow hats. Solberg, too, was chirpy, grateful for a drive in a third Focus. His boundless enthusiasm, and improving grasp of British humour, had made him a popular member of the team.

John Millington said: 'Petter used to wonder what all the jokes were about and what was going on, but he's caught on and now he's at the centre of everything. He's got the enthusiasm of youth. He listens and he does what he's told. He doesn't moan. That rubs off on people. He's good for all of us.'

Solberg was inevitably down in the hotel car park, where Ford's mechanics were making final checks on the three Focuses, long before his official start time in the town centre. McRae strolled out into the gentle sunshine, chatting to engineers, before returning to the hotel to top up his own fuel tank. Grist was reliving a driving success already achieved here. He beat all-comers with a shot of 262 metres on the golf course. Suddenly he realised time was pressing. 'Where's Colin? Go get him, will you.'

McRae duly reported for business and the pair made the short journey to the formal send-off, a sun-tanned Grist lounging back and acknowledging colleagues with a royal wave. A crowd of several hundred had gathered in the pedestrian precinct to

see the car mount the start ramp. The assembled were orderly and smiling. There was no sign of a policeman or steward, much less the need. Everything in Jyvaskyla that Friday afternoon was orderly and smiling. It could have been Trumpton.

The Finnish flag, carried by a smiling girl, and a round of applause accompanied the first local hero, Mäkinen, on to the ramp. Sainz earned 'whoops' from a besotted female. The next local hero, Kankkunen, benefited from the injection of emotion and received an almost fervent cheer. The flag of the Union rather than the Saltire led McRae forward. The announcer gave name checks to father Jimmy and brother Alister, then sent the Focus on its way. Solberg was further back in the field of 130, waiting his turn and talking on his mobile phone. 'Probably on to his girlfriend [also a competitor],' someone reckoned.

The message on the team radio link indicated a first concern for McRae, a problem with his windscreen wiper. Millington warned Gallagher and Mills to beware of faulty start-lights. McRae stumbled on the first stage, hitting a rock and stalling the engine. He was able to restart the motor and continue. Solberg's power steering played up on the third stage and added to the work schedule of the crew, positioned at the first service park, along a disused runway at Jyvaskyla Airport.

A row of motorhomes and vans stretched as far as the eye could see. Down at the amateur end it looked like a car boot sale. At the posh end armies of mechanics in uniform set out their tool kits in readiness for their cars. The support crews for the privateers had plenty of time to mingle and chat with their neighbours. One half of the Skoda operation was already packing up. Armin Schwarz had ripped off a wheel on the first stage. 'He's in for an ear bashing,' a seasoned observer suggested. McRae had avoided such embarrassment but was 11th. Solberg was 17th and Rådström a bullish fourth, having set the fastest time on stage two.

Ford had a team of nearly 60 to run their three-car operation and they became a blue blur of motion as first McRae, then Rådström, then Solberg, in the non-Martini car, rolled beneath their canopies. McRae's crew set about his car at a frantic pace, stiffening the settings. A subdued McRae and a buoyant Rådström sat in the modest motorhome used at this service, while Grist stood outside, re-enacting his winning drive for another listener.

Work on Solberg's car was more frantic still. The problem was traced to the centre diff. Wilson had a difficult decision to make. Time was pressing but he came to the conclusion they had to change the gearbox. Now mechanics were sprinting between the car and the van. With McRae gone, his men augmented the effort. Mechanics crowded under the car and tore away at the parts like scavenging hyenas at a carcass. The tense shouts of the crew heightened the drama. This was theatre. Wilson watched anxiously from the wings, checking his watch. Whitaker gazed in wide-eyed wonderment. He could have been a child at his first pantomime.

Look Colin, don't get me wrong, but I think you are over-driving

'This is the best bit for me,' he said. 'I could watch this all day. In the middle of winter the lads were having to work out what went where. Look at them now, and watch it all come together.'

They did not, of course, have all day. They had the engine running even before the job was done. A slight hitch at the front right cost them a few seconds but the car was down and away on time. They had changed the gearbox in $13\frac{1}{2}$ minutes. Wilson shook a clenched fist as if he had won the rally. Those watching from behind the tape applauded. It was a performance that deserved a bigger audience.

A cast of 12 had taken centre stage. 'Too many, to be honest,' Martin Wilkinson said. 'You can get in each other's way if you're not careful. But we got there. The boys did a great job.'

The excitement evidently got the better of Solberg. Millington radioed to Mills: 'Tell Petter to stop talking or he'll be late for the next stage.'

The crew hurried on to a service park on the edge of Jyvaskyla, which would be their base for the rest of the day. It seemed all Finland had joined them. Plus Rådström's barmy army. They gave him a raucous reception after the Swede claimed another fastest time on the final stage and consolidated his fourth place overall. McRae, second fastest on that short super special stage, was ninth overall, Solberg 15th.

'It's difficult to say how the car is now,' a still reticent McRae said. 'At least I've got a bit more confidence for tomorrow. But we'll have to see.'

Wilson had patently been disturbed by what he had seen on that opening day. He had taken his helicopter out on to the stages to form his own impression of proceedings. That night, in the hotel restaurant, he gently offered his senior driver words of advice and encouragement.

'I said to him, "Look Colin, don't get me wrong, but I think you're over-driving." And he said, "That's fair enough, you're right." It's all down to confidence. He's not got a good record here and he was aware of that. He'd got a bit of a psychological block over it. He needed to be more relaxed and positive about it and that's what I tried to get through to him.'

Saturday morning was crisp and clear enough to sort out anyone's head. This was to be the longest day of the rally, a journey deep into the forests and a meeting with those fast tracts and fearsome humps. Millington was instantly into his role as the sorting officer for team intelligence, passing information from the gravel crew to George Black, the appropriately named tyre man. Gallagher sent an alert about heavy traffic; Grist warned of a police radar trap.

Spectators had already claimed their vantage points on the first stage. Some had camped out overnight to secure their favoured spots. A tricky right-hander proved popular with fans of all ages. Seated at the front were a couple with their seven-month-old daughter, snug in a nest on her father's lap and seemingly entranced by the giant, snarling toys. She saw Mäkinen take a tight line, McRae opt for the wider, more spectacular route and Markko Martin almost lose it on a different, snaking course altogether, much to the amusement of the gallery. A veteran spectator in a bobble hat kept those about him up to speed with the stage times, courtesy of the excellent local radio service. By the time the top 20 had gone through, fans began to hurry away, and jump into their cars, only to be trapped in a hopeless traffic jam.

Ford's drivers had their own troubles. McRae was unhappy with the brakes, Rådström's drink bottle fell into the footwell and Solberg reported more steering problems.

Mills: 'We've lost all steering. Do you want us to carry on through?'

Millington: 'As long as there's no danger of fire.'

Solberg struggled through the stage, three minutes off the pace. Jimmy McRae informed his son the second stage was 'similar to the previous stage, generally drying out.' Road signs warned of elks, but they obviously had the good sense to steer clear of the motorfest. Besides, they had a vast, uninhabited wilderness to themselves. This is, indeed, a country of lakes, but also of forests. Silver birch, as well as firs, fill the landscape.

As McRae and the rest cut their way through the latest tree-lined test, his crew were doctoring tyres for the next section. Nothing sophisticated about the technique here. They simply hacked chunks out of the rubber. McRae, meanwhile, was lopping seconds off the leaders. The team had word he was second quickest on that stage. A different brake system doubtless helped restore his confidence, but perhaps Wilson's counselling was working also.

Elaine Wilson beamed a smile of relief. Solberg talked of the 'family' atmosphere and that is apparent. Elaine organises the team gear, provided by Martini, and cheerfully fills the role of agony aunt. 'The boys will come to me with their problems, most of which Malcolm doesn't know about and doesn't need to know about,' she says. Not that she is a soft

An unusually reticent McRae.

McRae begins to see the light.

touch. When a mechanic tries it on and claims he needs a new pair of trousers after a couple of rallies he is likely to be sent packing with a flea in his ear. Son Matthew, on school holiday, also joined the team here. By all accounts he is well on the way to emulating his father as both a driver and a manager.

McRae required no arm around him when he came into the service park at Orivesi. He had a better feeling for the car and was up to seventh. 'I'm starting to get fired up,' he said. Now Rådström had the haunted look. He could not understand why he hadn't reproduced the speed of the previous day. He was down to sixth. The technicians on Solberg's car diagnosed a sensor failure, so there was more up-tempo activity on the white Focus.

Grist was able to enjoy the break. 'Colin's definitely getting more confident. When your confidence is down you lose ten per cent horsepower. His basic problem here is a lack of match practice, but he's getting that now.'

Wilson, pad in hand, jumper around his shoulders, made for a waiting car and was driven to the edge of town, where his helicopter was ready to airlift him to the next stage. He has a pilot's licence but employs a full-time pilot, Norman Osment, an ex-Army man and a former amateur rally dri-

ver. The view from the helicopter confirmed the ground-level impression: Finland is a country of water and trees. Small islands dot the lakes like flotsam. Wooden summerhouses hug the shores.

Osment swooped over the stage and put down in a clearing designated as one of the official landing points on this chopper friendly rally. Thirty-two helicopters were registered for the event. Eleven were parked here.

'Believe it or not, this is the first time I've done this, spectating,' Wilson said. 'It gives me a chance to see the cars on the stage and that's why I was able to go to Colin and tell him what I thought last night. What you do realise is that there is so little difference between the cars now.'

Among the privileged gathering was Ari Vatanen, driver-turned-European-politician and a celebrity in either guise. 'This is the way to watch rallying,' he said. 'People having picnics, plenty of space, good view of the cars. I'm not officially retired from driving but I gave up on a call from you a long time ago, Malcolm.'

Wilson tapped his heart in mock relief.

Vatanen: 'How's Colin?'

Wilson: 'OK. He wants to finish this one. He's not done that since his first one here – with you!'

Marcus Gronholm, the overnight leader, was the first to appear from behind the trees, drop and veer right in one aggressive but controlled movement. Two telegraph poles on the left side of the road assured his fullest concentration. The Peugeot straightened up to take a narrow bridge over a ditch and then accelerated out of sight.

Most of the front-runners were quick or at least efficient. With the notable exception of Auriol. 'No, no, no,' exclaimed Vatanen as the Frenchman vainly wrestled with his recalcitrant Toyota all over the road.

A more cynical bystander said: 'The stage must be 300 metres longer for him.'

Wilson watched his drivers safely through and turned towards his helicopter to fly to the next stage.

'I know a good place,' Vatanen intervened. 'It's a private place, a farm. Best place on the stage. I go to a lot of these farmhouses. They say they remember me from 20 years ago. I stayed a little too long for coffee at the last one. Follow me.'

Wilson was happy to accept the invitation and Norman was instructed to follow that helicopter. They arced over a lake and came down in a narrower clearing. Here was a more earthy crowd; genuine rally fans, fortified with liquid refreshment. They exchanged banter with Vatanen, who marched past a pancake stall towards the farm buildings. A tractor trailer provided the optimum position for those lucky enough to have claimed their places. They saw the cars plunge, sweep and climb, all at mind-numbing speed.

The longest stage of the rally was always liable to claim its victims and it chose some of the most illustrious. The voice on the radio solemnly informed his listeners that Mäkinen had stopped. It would be revealed later he had a broken transmission. There was bad news for Wilson, too. Rådström, who impressed his boss passing the farm, went off further along the stage. Spectators helped him back on but he had to reduce his speed and lost around 12 minutes. McRae had difficulty hearing Grist's calls because of an intercom fault but he moved up to fifth. Thirteen seconds covered the top four, led by Kankkunen.

Wilson's helicopter climbed the wall of trees and turned towards the next service, flying over huge galleries on the stage. As it landed Grist was asking Millington to repeat the name of 'that Finnish driver'. A smiling Wilson explained: 'Nicky's winding up Milli again.'

The Yorkshireman's pronunciation has earned him minor cult status.

Less amusing was the state of Rådström's car and his mechanics hammered at the hatch to get it back into shape. McRae, with normal in-car communications restored, was fastest on the next stage. He returned to service and the approval of his boss. 'It was as if you were on rails,' Wilson said.

McRae had his ego buffed up a little more on the following road section. Two

DIY job for Rådström.

women held up a banner urging, 'Go Colin, Go.' He missed the one displayed a couple of kilometres down the road. It read, 'Waik up, Colin'. Grist was more observant and gleefully told his partner. 'Cheeky wee bastards,' McRae growled.

The pair became preoccupied with the clock. Heavy traffic put them six minutes behind schedule and the team had more warnings of those wretched radar traps. McRae tucked in behind two other rally cars ducking in and out of the normal traffic and made up the time.

Millington was still reading out the stage times. Wilkinson queried: 'What was the name of that local guy again?'

An unflustered Millington replied: 'How did I know you were going to ask me that?'

Drizzle welcomed the competitors to the closing stages, two more runs of the short Hippos. McRae was fastest and joint fastest, finishing the day fourth overall. Solberg was 16th and Rådström 22nd.

Solberg was near delirious after maintaining his confident advance the following morning. 'The car is so good it is almost better than having sex,' he yelled at a startled radio interviewer.

McRae's reluctant love affair with Finland turned sour again on the penultimate stage. He had a problem. 'I think it might be a piston,' he said.

Grist came in: 'Do you want us to retire?'

Millington: 'If it's terminal, yes. If not, no.'

Millington followed up with a firm instruction: 'Nicky, check in as normal and let Martin see it.'

McRae: 'It's still running. Sounds like a piston.'

Wilkinson: 'I'll be down there to see you.'

The problem relegated McRae to sixth but a point still beckoned, as long as he could keep going through the final 'TV special' test. Rådström had already formally retired from the rally but would, along with Mäkinen and Auriol, take the opportunity to compete for bonus points.

Whole battalions of fans were tramping through the soft flora of the forest floor for a view of the stage. A TV cameraman, positioned just beyond a crest, wore an ice-hockey player's helmet. The blue and yellow hats of Rådström's fans were visible through the trees.

McRae finally gets the measure of Finland's jumps.

Dark clouds seemed inexorably drawn to the action as Mäkinen set off. The speed trap on the crest showed 138kph, to the roars of the gallery. Rådström registered 136 but it was Auriol, with 134, who went on to achieve the fastest time on the stage and claim three Championship points.

Rain called for caution from the later runners but that was the least of McRae's worries. He was comfortably on course for sixth place overall when the engine began to seize. The speed trap crept to 40, then slipped back to 30, 20, 15 and finally a blank screen confirmed the worst. Steam rose from the stationary Focus, to unsympathetic cheers. The mood of the spectators changed when McRae and Grist abandoned their stricken car. They applauded warmly as the pair set off walking to the end of the stage – a distance of a mere 600 metres.

Kankkunen went through to win his home rally and a record 23rd in World Championship competition. Burns was second, Sainz third. Solberg was 12th.

Mäkinen's two points from the TV show put him on 48, 10 ahead of Auriol, in second place. McRae was sixth, 25 points behind the leader.

'It was worth a try for a point and we almost made it but the engine just died,' McRae said. 'At least we've done all the stages.'

Solberg returned to the final service point to an ovation from his crew. 'I couldn't think it would go so well,' he shrieked. 'I was afraid of the jumps like hell. But they were not so bad. Now I'm really looking forward to next year.'

Wilson faced the cameras. 'We've had five fastest stage times, so that's something positive to take from the rally,' he reasoned. 'I would be worried if we weren't competitive. It's the first serious engine problem we've had this season, and remember this is one of the world's fastest rallies, with the engine running at high revs for a long time. What we have to do is get rid of the gremlins. Colin has to be a favourite for China because he knows the stages better than any other of the top drivers. But we've got to improve the reliability to fulfil the potential.'

Rådström and Gallagher leaving the start ramp for their ill-fated drive in China.

The team had sent food and water by ship from New Zealand to China ahead of the event. McRae's campaign was in urgent need of sustenance.

By the time the World Rally Championship circus arrived at the Great Wall, Mäkinen had decided to stay at Mitsubishi and Ford were spared further conjecture about the consequences of pairing the Finn with McRae. They had other matters to occupy them. The team needed to eliminate the problems that had hounded them through the summer and continue their development of a lighter car, particularly with San Remo in mind.

McRae planned to tone up for China's World Championship debut with a lengthy cycling stint, but torrential rain intervened. It was not the first time extreme elements had interrupted McRae's training schedule here. On a previous visit, for a non-title event, he was struck by lightning as he, Grist and Muckle were jogging by the Great Wall. 'It was as if someone punched me at the back of the head,' McRae recalled. 'The lightning seemed to rebound off the Wall.' The force lowered McRae to his knees but he lifted himself and carried on. Little wonder he no longer cares for jogging.

McRae had to pick himself up now and at least he was able to glean encouragement from his experiences driving a car in these parts. He won the rally in 1997 and 1998, albeit against modest opposition, and on the face of it had a useful advantage over his recognised rivals, for whom this was unfamiliar ground.

'It helps but it isn't the type of event where experience counts for much from a driving point of view,' McRae cautioned. 'The roads are narrow, hilly in places and quite similar to Portugal. It's a rally which a first-timer can win.'

Wilson was grateful for the benefit of McRae's wider knowledge of China. 'Colin's understanding of the roads means he's been able to advise us on the event and the specification we should use for the cars. He and Nicky have also been invaluable in other areas by explaining what we can expect in terms of different cultures,

McRae's brief encounter with the China Rally.

language difficulties, food and making the team function in the usual fashion.'

Gallagher, too, was able to contribute to the intelligence file. Although these stages were new to him he had competed on the Hong Kong–Beijing Rally three times – winning the 1987 event – and on the Paris–Beijing Rally in 1992. He said: 'Because there's been little motorised traffic in China until relatively recently, there's no real signposting, and where there are signs they are obviously in Chinese. Away from the major towns nobody speaks English, so stopping to ask the way is pointless. I think it will be an adventure, in some ways a throwback to the old days of the sport, and I just hope the organisers will allow the character of the country to come through so that it doesn't appear like just another European round.'

The rally, based in Huai Rou, about 60 kilometres north of Beijing, was due to be given a ceremonial evening send-off but that, along with the two longest stages of the first day proper, had to be cancelled because of the rain. Ford's interest was washed away a mere two kilometres into the opening test. McRae hit concrete protruding on the inside of a right-hand bend, the impact damaging his suspension and compelling him to retire. Astonishingly, Rådström struck the same unforgiving obstacle minutes later and suffered the same fate.

McRae said: 'We noted the concrete during the recce but didn't think it was a major hazard. Approaching the bend we could see tyre marks where the earlier cars had driven over it. We ran over it and unfortunately damaged the suspension too badly to continue. I think the rain had washed away the earth around the concrete and it was sticking up more than it had been in the recce.'

An equally dismayed Rådström said: 'It was Unbelievable – with a capital U! As I approached the bend I could see Colin stopped 200 metres ahead and knew something was wrong. It was a slow corner and we were in second gear because there was a tight left-hand bend just afterwards so we had to slow down. We drove over the concrete and that was it. This is hard for Colin, hard for me, hard for the team.'

If Wilson was pushed to the point of despair he rallied with admirable stoicism. He instructed engineers and technicians to reinforce the suspension of the Focus and detailed Rådström to test the car the following day.

In more senses than one the China Rally was a watershed for Ford. It marked the end of any lingering hopes of winning the 1999 World Championship and the beginning of the concerted campaign for success in 2000. McRae and the team were intent on finishing their first season together with a flourish, and no driver anticipated the concluding round, in Britain, more eagerly. However, the real challenge lay further ahead, at Monte Carlo and beyond. The lessons of the past months would enhance their operation and strengthen their resolve to realise that Championship objective.

Index

Pictures are indicated by **bold** type